Blackstone
Outdoor Griddle
Cookbook

Ted Gibbs

GET YOUR 5 BLACKSTONE BONUSES

 SCAN HERE TO DOWNLOAD IT

Contents

Baked Ziti 98

Margherita Pizza 98

Vegetarian Pizza 99

Carbonara Spaghetti 99

Fettuccine Alfredo 99

Garlic Shrimp Linguine 100

Creamy Chicken and Broccoli Alfredo 100

Pepperoni Pizza 101

BBQ Chicken Pizza 101

Four Cheese Pizza 101

Tomato and Basil Spaghetti 101

Conclusion: 102

Introduction:

Welcome to the Blackstone Griddle Cookbook! Embrace the excitement and versatility of cooking on a Blackstone Griddle. This cookbook is a treasure trove of over 200 recipes, ranging from breakfast favorites to exquisite pizza and pasta creations. The Blackstone Griddle, a modern take on traditional cooking methods, revolutionizes outdoor cooking. With its large, flat surface, it's a fantastic tool for enhancing the natural flavors of ingredients, creating distinct and delightful tastes that grilling enthusiasts love.

Whether you're a seasoned griddle aficionado or new to the world of flat top cooking, this cookbook is designed to guide you through the art of griddle cooking. Here, you'll discover a wide array of dishes including breakfast and brunch delights, appetizers, side dishes, salads, vegetarian options, seafood, burgers, chicken, pork, beef, and even pizza and pasta dishes - all tailored for your Blackstone Griddle.

Every recipe in this collection comes with clear, step-by-step instructions and detailed ingredient lists. We've also included valuable tips and tricks to help you make the most of your griddle. From mastering the perfect temperature settings for various foods to understanding the benefits of cooking on a flat top, this cookbook is your comprehensive guide to becoming a Blackstone Griddle master.

Cooking on a Blackstone Griddle is not only convenient but also a healthier way to prepare meals. The griddle's design allows for less oil usage, contributing to overall calorie reduction. Enjoy cooking a diverse range of recipes that are both delicious and healthy, catering to all taste preferences. From classic American-style burgers to sophisticated Italian pasta dishes, the Blackstone Griddle Cookbook offers something for every palate, whether you're preparing a family meal or hosting a festive outdoor gathering.

Let the Blackstone Griddle Cookbook be your essential guide to exploring the culinary possibilities of griddle cooking. With its plethora of delectable and easy-to-follow recipes, this book is set to become an indispensable resource in your cooking repertoire.

Now, let's fire up that griddle and embark on a flavorful journey!

The Rising Popularity of Blackstone Griddle Cooking

Blackstone Griddle cooking is gaining momentum in the world of outdoor cuisine, and it's easy to see why. Cooking on a Blackstone Griddle offers a range of benefits and features that make it an increasingly preferred method for many culinary enthusiasts. In this section, we'll explore the advantages and unique aspects of cooking on a Blackstone Griddle, highlighting why it might be the perfect choice for your outdoor culinary adventures.

Ease of Use

One of the primary advantages of cooking on a Blackstone Griddle is its ease of use. Blackstone Griddles heat up quickly and maintain consistent heat, perfect for spontaneous outdoor feasts or casual gatherings. Unlike traditional charcoal grills, there's no need for a lengthy setup or waiting for coals to reach the right temperature, allowing more time to relish your meals and company. Additionally, the flat top surface offers ample space for cooking multiple items simultaneously, streamlining the entire cooking process.

Precise Temperature Control

Another key benefit of the Blackstone Griddle is the precision in temperature control. Unlike charcoal grills, which can be challenging to regulate, Blackstone Griddles allow for specific temperature adjustments, providing you with more control over your cooking. This precise control facilitates even cooking and reduces the chances of under or overcooking your food. It's also easier to create different heat zones for versatile cooking methods on the expansive griddle surface.

Versatility

The Blackstone Griddle shines in its versatility. It's not just for grilling burgers or hot dogs; it's also perfect for cooking delicate items like eggs, pancakes, fish, and vegetables. The flat surface accommodates a variety of cooking techniques, including sautéing, toasting, and even simmering. This versatility makes the Blackstone Griddle an excellent choice for those who love experimenting with different cuisines and cooking styles.

Healthier Cooking Options

Cooking on a Blackstone Griddle can be a healthier option compared to other methods. The flat top design allows for cooking with less oil, and excess grease can be easily scraped off, reducing the overall fat content of your meals. This results in healthier, less greasy food while still retaining all the flavor.

Time Efficiency

Blackstone Griddles are incredibly efficient. They reach the desired temperature quickly and cook food faster than traditional grills. This efficiency means you spend less time cooking and more time enjoying your dishes. The spacious cooking surface also allows for preparing multiple food items at once, further saving time.

Safety and Ease of Operation

Finally, Blackstone Griddles are designed with safety and simplicity in mind. Their stable design reduces the risk of tipping or accidents associated with open flames. Starting, operating, and cleaning the griddle is straightforward, making it a hassle-free option for any cookout. Additionally, their robust build and easy-to-maintain surface ensure a safe and enjoyable cooking experience.

In conclusion, cooking on a Blackstone Griddle brings numerous advantages, making it a fantastic choice for outdoor dining experiences. With its convenience, precision, versatility, healthier cooking options, efficiency, and safety, the Blackstone Griddle is a dynamic and effective tool for creating delicious, nutritious meals for both large gatherings and intimate family dinners.

Tips and Tricks for Preparing and Using the Blackstone Griddle

Cooking on a Blackstone Griddle offers a unique and enjoyable way to prepare a wide variety of dishes outdoors. To get the most out of your griddle experience, it's important to understand the best practices for preparation and use. This section covers essential tips and tricks for using your Blackstone Griddle, including temperature management, griddle placement, and cleaning.

Temperature Management

Effective temperature control is crucial for achieving perfect results on the Blackstone Griddle. Before starting your cooking, it's important to preheat the griddle. A general guideline is to heat the griddle for 10-15 minutes, which ensures even cooking and helps retain the moisture of the food.

For precise temperature monitoring, consider using an infrared thermometer. While the Blackstone Griddle has built-in heat controls, an infrared thermometer can help you ensure the griddle is at the perfect temperature for whatever you're cooking, from pancakes to steaks.

Griddle Placement

Strategically placing your food on the griddle surface is key. Unlike grills, the griddle provides a uniform cooking area, but understanding where your griddle tends to be hotter (usually the center) can help in cooking foods more effectively. For example, sear meats in the hotter zones and cook vegetables or more delicate items in cooler areas.

Keeping your griddle surface clean and lightly oiled is essential. Before cooking, use a griddle scraper to remove any residue. Applying a light layer of cooking oil helps create a non-stick surface and adds flavor to your food.

Cleaning

Maintaining your Blackstone Griddle involves regular cleaning to preserve its performance and longevity. After each use, use a griddle scraper to remove debris. Then, wipe down the surface with a cloth or paper towel. For thorough cleaning, use a mild detergent and water, but ensure the griddle is completely dry to prevent rusting.

Propane Safety

If your Blackstone Griddle uses propane, it's important to handle it safely. Always turn off the propane tank and griddle controls after use. Never leave the griddle unattended when it's on. If you detect a gas smell or suspect a leak, immediately turn off the gas and seek professional help.

Accessories

Enhance your Blackstone Griddle experience with the right accessories. Essential tools like spatulas, scrapers, and tongs are vital for effective cooking. Additional items like squeeze bottles for oils and seasonings, griddle covers, and cleaning kits can further improve your cooking process.

Conclusion

By mastering these tips and tricks, you can make the most of your Blackstone Griddle cooking experience. Temperature management, strategic food placement, regular cleaning, safety precautions, and the right accessories are key to successful and enjoyable griddle cooking. With these practices, you're well on your way to creating a multitude of delicious, perfectly-cooked meals on your Blackstone Griddle.

Cleaning Your Blackstone Griddle Properly for Optimal Performance and Longevity

Maintaining a clean griddle is essential not just for appearance but also for ensuring it cooks effectively and safely. This section will provide you with 15 cleaning tips specifically tailored for your Blackstone Griddle, covering both routine and deep cleaning tasks.

Scrape the Griddle Surface
The most important part of cleaning your Blackstone Griddle is the cooking surface. Use a flat griddle scraper to remove debris or residue before and after each use. For tougher grime, a griddle cleaning solution or a mixture of vinegar and water can be effective.

Soak Stubborn Residue
If there are stubborn food residues, you can lightly soak the surface with warm water and a gentle detergent. This can help soften the grime, making it easier to scrape off.

Use a Grease Management System
Your Blackstone Griddle includes a grease management system to capture and dispose of excess grease. Ensure it's emptied and cleaned after each use to prevent buildup and potential flare-ups.

Clean Underneath the Griddle
Regularly lift the griddle plate and clean underneath. Debris and grease can accumulate here and potentially affect the performance of your griddle.

Maintain the Burners
If your griddle has burners, ensure they are free from debris and grease. A brush or cloth can be used to gently clean them.

Clean the Exterior
The griddle's exterior should also be kept clean. Wipe down the exterior surfaces with a damp cloth or gentle cleaning solution to keep it looking pristine.

Manage Grease Disposal
Properly dispose of grease collected in the grease trap. Regular cleaning of the trap is necessary to maintain hygiene and griddle performance.

Use a Griddle Cover
Protect your Blackstone Griddle from the elements and reduce the buildup of dust and debris by using a cover. Make sure the cover is clean and dry before using.

Maintain Cleaning Tools
Keep your griddle scrapers, brushes, and sponges clean. Regularly wash them with soap and water, replacing them when they wear out.

Choose Safe Cleaning Products
Always opt for non-toxic, griddle-safe cleaners. This ensures no harmful chemicals are left behind that could contaminate your food.

Wear Protective Gear
When undertaking deep cleaning, wear gloves and, if necessary, eye protection to keep yourself safe from grease and cleaning products.

Consider Using a Mild Power Washing
For deep cleaning, a gentle power wash can be effective, especially for removing tough grime. Be cautious with water pressure to avoid damage to the griddle.

Regular Cleaning Schedule
Adopt a regular cleaning routine. A clean griddle after each use and periodic deep cleanings can prolong its life and maintain its performance.

Professional Maintenance
If you're unsure about certain aspects of cleaning your griddle, don't hesitate to seek professional help. A seasoned technician can offer deep cleaning and maintenance services.

Season the Griddle
After cleaning, it's important to season the griddle surface. This involves heating it and applying a thin layer of oil to create a non-stick surface and prevent rust.

Recommended accessories and equipment

Using the right accessories and equipment can significantly improve your experience with the Blackstone Griddle. In this section, we'll discuss some of the best accessories and equipment tailored for griddle cooking.

Griddle Scraper

A good griddle scraper is essential for keeping the flat top clean. Look for one with a sturdy blade and a comfortable handle for efficient cleaning.

Long-Handled Spatulas

Long-handled spatulas are indispensable for safely moving and flipping food on the hot griddle surface. Choose spatulas that are durable and designed specifically for griddle use.

Griddle Cover

A cover is essential for protecting your Blackstone Griddle from the elements. Look for a cover that is weather-resistant and fits your griddle model snugly.

Heat-Resistant Gloves

Heat-resistant gloves are crucial for handling hot utensils or the griddle itself. Choose gloves that offer both heat resistance and a good grip.

Griddle Accessory Kit

A griddle accessory kit, typically including spatulas, choppers, and squeeze bottles, can make managing food on the griddle easier. Opt for a set that offers versatility and durability.

Vegetable Baskets

While primarily for grilling, vegetable baskets can also be useful on a griddle for containing smaller items or for stir-frying. Choose baskets with handles and nonstick surfaces.

Seasoning Oils and Sprays

High-quality oils and sprays are key for seasoning and cooking on the griddle. Look for nonstick sprays or high-smoke-point oils for the best cooking experience.

LED Griddle Light

A griddle light can be helpful for cooking in low-light conditions. Select a light that easily attaches to your griddle and provides ample illumination.

Griddle Cleaning Kit

A griddle cleaning kit with cleaning pads, scrapers, and solutions designed for griddle surfaces will help maintain your griddle in top condition.

Infrared Thermometer

An infrared thermometer is helpful for checking the surface temperature of your griddle, ensuring optimal cooking conditions. Look for one with a wide temperature range and durable construction.

Griddle Press

A griddle press is great for making perfectly seared burgers or paninis. Choose a press that is heavy enough to provide a good sear without being cumbersome.

Griddle Dome

A dome cover can be used to create a steamy environment for melting cheese on burgers or cooking vegetables faster. Opt for a dome that's large enough to cover multiple items at once.

Non-Stick Griddle Mats

Non-stick mats can be used on your griddle for cooking delicate items like eggs or fish. Ensure they are designed for high-heat cooking and are easy to clean.

Portable Cooler

For outdoor griddle cooking, a portable cooler or ice chest is useful for keeping ingredients fresh. Choose one that is easy to transport and has sufficient capacity.

Pizza Stone

A pizza stone can be used on the griddle for cooking pizzas with a crispy crust. Look for a stone that is suitable for high heat and fits comfortably on your griddle.

In conclusion, selecting the right accessories and equipment can greatly enhance your cooking experience on the Blackstone Griddle. High-quality, griddle-specific accessories will not only make cooking more enjoyable but also contribute to the longevity and maintenance of your griddle.

Breakfast and Brunch

Cornmeal pancakes

Portion Size: 2
Duration: 45 minutes

Ingredients:
3/4 cup cornmeal
1/2 cup + 2 tbsp flour
1/4 tsp baking soda
1/2 tsp salt
1 cup buttermilk
1 egg
2 tbsp butter, melted (or 4 tbsp margarine)

Instructions:
In a mixing bowl, combine cornmeal, flour, baking soda, and salt.

In another bowl, whisk together the buttermilk and egg.

Gradually add the dry ingredients to the wet ingredients, mixing until just combined. Stir in melted butter.

Preheat your Blackstone Griddle to medium heat and lightly oil the surface.

Pour batter onto the griddle to form pancakes. Cook until bubbles appear on the surface, then flip and cook until golden brown.

Serve hot with syrup of your choice.

Nutrition Facts (1 portion):
Energy: 472 Kcal
Carbs: 61g
Proteins: 15g
Fats: 19g

Denver Omelet Salad

Portion Size: 2
Duration: 25 minutes

Ingredients:
4 cups fresh baby spinach
1/2 cup chopped tomatoes
1 tbsp olive oil
1 cup cooked and chopped ham
1 small onion, diced
1 small green pepper, diced
2 large eggs
Salt and pepper to taste

Instructions:
Place spinach and tomatoes in a salad bowl and set aside.

Preheat your Blackstone Griddle to medium-high heat. Add half the olive oil, onions, and green peppers, and cook for about 5 minutes until soft.

Add the chopped ham and continue cooking until the ham is heated through, about 2 minutes.

Add the cooked ham mixture to the salad bowl with spinach and tomatoes.

Using the same griddle, warm the remaining oil. Crack the eggs into small cups and gently slide them onto the griddle. Season with salt and pepper.

Cook the eggs sunny-side-up to your preferred doneness.

Top the salad with the fried eggs and serve.

Nutrition Facts (1 portion):
Energy: 229 Kcal
Carbs: 7g
Proteins: 20g
Fats: 14g

Savory Breakfast Skillet

Portion Size: 2
Duration: 25 min

Ingredients:
1/2 lb diced red potatoes
1/2 cup diced bell peppers
1/2 cup diced onions
4 oz cooked breakfast sausage, crumbled
4 large eggs
Salt and pepper to taste
1/2 cup shredded cheddar cheese
1 tbsp olive oil

Instructions:
Preheat the Blackstone griddle to medium-high heat and add olive oil.

Add potatoes, bell peppers, and onions to the griddle. Cook for about 10 minutes until potatoes are tender and slightly crispy.

Add the crumbled sausage to the griddle and cook for another 5 minutes.

Create wells in the mixture and crack an egg into each well. Season with salt and pepper.

Cover and cook until eggs are set to your desired doneness.

Sprinkle with cheddar cheese and serve directly from the griddle.

Nutrition Facts (1 portion):
Energy: 520 Kcal
Carbs: 40g
Proteins: 28g
Fats: 28g

S'mores Waffle Sandwich

Portion Size: 2
Duration: 10 minutes

Ingredients:
1 frozen waffle
Half a milk chocolate bar, broken into pieces
1/4 cup miniature marshmallows

Instructions:
Preheat the Blackstone Griddle to medium heat.

Place the waffle on the griddle and cook for about 4 minutes until crisp.

Top one waffle half with chocolate pieces and marshmallows.

Cover with the other waffle half and press gently.

Cook for an additional minute until the chocolate melts.

Nutrition Facts (1 serving):
Energy: 62 Kcal
Carbs: 9.29g
Proteins: 1.21g
Fats: 2.28g

Griddle Pancake Stack with Bacon

Portion Size: 2
Duration: 30 min

Ingredients:
1 cup all-purpose flour
2 tbsp sugar
1 tsp baking powder
1/2 tsp baking soda
1/4 tsp salt
1 cup buttermilk

1 egg

2 tbsp unsalted butter, melted

6 slices bacon

Maple syrup for serving

Instructions:

In a bowl, mix flour, sugar, baking powder, baking soda, and salt.

In another bowl, whisk together buttermilk, egg, and melted butter.

Combine the wet ingredients with the dry ingredients until just mixed.

Preheat the Blackstone griddle over medium heat and cook bacon until crispy. Set aside.

Pour 1/4 cup batter for each pancake onto the griddle. Cook until bubbles form on the surface, then flip and cook until golden.

Serve pancakes in a stack with bacon on the side and maple syrup.

Nutrition Facts (1 portion):

Energy: 575 Kcal

Carbs: 60g

Proteins: 20g

Fats: 28g

Grilled Chicken Pita

Portion Size: 2

Duration: 30 minutes

Ingredients:

1/2 lb skinless, boneless chicken thighs

1/2 cup Lemon & Garlic Marinade

Salt and pepper to taste

1/2 tsp olive oil

1/2 lb Organic Hearty Grain Pita, split

4 Tbsp Tzatziki Dip, divided

1 plum tomato, diced, or 4 Cherry Tomatoes, quartered

1/4 onion, diced

1/2 cucumber, diced

Optional: Feta Cheese, crumbled

Instructions:

Marinate chicken in lemon and garlic marinade for 12-24 hours in the fridge.

Preheat the Blackstone Griddle to medium-high heat.

Season chicken with salt, pepper, and a light coating of olive oil.

Cook chicken on the griddle for about 9-10 minutes until the internal temperature reaches 155°F, then let it rest until it reaches 165°F.

Slice the chicken.

Warm the pitas on the griddle for about a minute.

Spread 2 tbsp of tzatziki on each pita, then top with chicken, onion, cucumber, and tomatoes.

Sprinkle with feta cheese if desired.

Nutrition Facts (1 portion):

Energy: 560 Kcal

Carbs: 46g

Proteins: 34g

Fats: 30g

Savory Hot Cereal with Apple

Portion Size: 2

Duration: 15 minutes

Ingredients:

1 medium Ginger Gold or Granny Smith apple

1 1/2 cups water

1/2 tbsp Basting Oil

2.5 oz instant cream of wheat cereal

1/4 cup Grated Grana Padano Cheese

Pepper to taste

Salt to taste

Instructions:

Grate one apple and slice thinly.

In a pot on the griddle, combine grated apple, water, and basting oil. Bring to a boil.

In a bowl, mix cream of wheat with Grana Padano Cheese.

Pour the hot apple-water mixture into the bowl. Stir for a minute until thickened.

Season with salt and pepper to taste.

Serve in warm bowls, topped with apple slices.

Nutrition Facts (1 portion):

Energy: 260 Kcal

Carbs: 40g

Proteins: 8g

Fats: 7g

Griddle Hash Browns with Smoked Salmon

Portion Size: 2

Duration: 25 min

Ingredients:

2 cups shredded potatoes (rinsed and drained)

4 oz smoked salmon

2 tbsp chopped dill

2 tbsp olive oil

1/4 cup sour cream

1 lemon, sliced

Salt and pepper to taste

Instructions:

Preheat the Blackstone griddle to medium-high heat.

Toss the shredded potatoes with salt, pepper, and 1 tbsp of olive oil.

Spread the potatoes on the griddle and press them down. Cook until golden and crispy on one side, then flip and cook the other side.

Serve the crispy hash browns with smoked salmon on top.

Add a dollop of sour cream on each serving and garnish with chopped dill and a lemon slice.

Nutrition Facts (1 portion):

Energy: 360 Kcal

Carbs: 42g

Proteins: 15g

Fats: 16g

Simple Scrambled Eggs

Portion Size: 2

Duration: 15 minutes

Ingredients:

4 Large Eggs

4 Tbsp 2% Reduced Fat Milk

Salt to taste

Cooking Spray

Instructions:

In a bowl, whisk together eggs, milk, and a pinch of salt.

Preheat the Blackstone Griddle to medium heat and coat with cooking spray.

Pour the egg mixture onto the griddle.

Cook for 3-4 minutes, stirring constantly with a spatula until the eggs are scrambled.

Season with salt and pepper, then serve.

Nutrition Facts (1 portion):

Energy: 160 Kcal

Carbs: 2g

Proteins: 13g

Fats: 11g

Griddle Veggie Omelette

Portion Size: 2

Duration: 15 min

Ingredients:

4 large eggs

1/4 cup diced tomatoes

1/4 cup chopped spinach

1/4 cup sliced mushrooms

1/4 cup shredded cheese (your choice)

2 tbsp milk

Salt and pepper to taste

1 tbsp butter

Instructions:

In a bowl, whisk together eggs, milk, salt, and pepper.

Preheat the Blackstone griddle to medium heat and add butter.

Pour half the egg mixture onto the griddle, tilting to spread evenly. Cook until the eggs start to set.

Sprinkle half the tomatoes, spinach, mushrooms, and cheese over one side of the omelette.

Gently fold the omelette in half and cook until the cheese melts.

Repeat with the remaining ingredients for the second omelette.

Serve hot.

Nutrition Facts (1 portion):

Energy: 290 Kcal

Carbs: 5g

Proteins: 20g

Fats: 21g

Griddle French Toast with Berry Compote

Portion Size: 2

Duration: 20 min

Ingredients:

4 slices of thick bread (like brioche or challah)

2 large eggs

1/2 cup milk

1 tsp vanilla extract

1/2 tsp cinnamon

2 tbsp butter

1 cup mixed berries (fresh or frozen)

2 tbsp maple syrup

Powdered sugar for dusting

Instructions:

In a bowl, whisk together eggs, milk, vanilla extract, and cinnamon.

Dip each bread slice into the egg mixture, ensuring both sides are well coated.

Heat 1 tbsp butter on the Blackstone griddle over medium heat.

Place the soaked bread slices on the griddle and cook until golden brown on each side.

In a separate area of the griddle, cook the mixed berries until they release their juices. Stir in maple syrup to create a compote.

Serve the French toast hot, topped with berry compote and a dusting of powdered sugar.

Nutrition Facts (1 portion):
Energy: 435 Kcal
Carbs: 57g
Proteins: 14g
Fats: 18g

Griddle Avocado Toast with Poached Eggs

Portion Size: 2
Duration: 15 min

Ingredients:
4 slices of whole-grain bread
2 ripe avocados, mashed
4 eggs
1 tbsp white vinegar
Salt and pepper to taste
Crushed red pepper flakes (optional)
Fresh herbs for garnish (like chives or parsley)

Instructions:
Toast the bread slices on the Blackstone griddle until crispy.

Spread mashed avocado on each slice of toast.

In a pan of simmering water with 1 tbsp of white vinegar, gently crack the eggs and poach to desired doneness.

Place a poached egg on each avocado toast.

Season with salt, pepper, and red pepper flakes.

Garnish with fresh herbs and serve.

Nutrition Facts (1 portion):
Energy: 370 Kcal
Carbs: 36g
Proteins: 15g
Fats: 20g

Roasted Asparagus with Parmigiano-Reggiano

Portion Size: 2
Duration: 20 minutes

Ingredients:
1 lb Asparagus, trimmed
2 Tbsp Olive Oil
2 Tbsp Grated Parmigiano Reggiano
Salt and Pepper to taste

Instructions:
Preheat the Blackstone Griddle to medium-high.

Toss asparagus with olive oil in a bowl.

Lay asparagus on the griddle and cook for about 15 mins until tender and slightly browned.

Sprinkle with Parmigiano Reggiano, salt, and pepper.

Cook for an additional 5 mins until the cheese softens.

Nutrition Facts (1 portion):
Energy: 130 Kcal
Carbs: 4g
Proteins: 4g
Fats: 12g

Crunchy French Toast

Portion Size: 2
Duration: 20 minutes

Ingredients:
3 Large Eggs
1/4 cup Fat-Free Milk
1 tsp Vanilla Extract
1/4 tsp Salt

1/2 cup Crushed Frosted Cornflakes

1/2 cup Old-Fashioned Oats

1/2 cup Sliced Almonds

4 slices Whole Wheat Bread

Maple Syrup for topping

Instructions:

In a bowl, whisk together eggs, milk, vanilla, and salt.

In another bowl, combine cornflakes, oats, and almonds.

Preheat the Blackstone Griddle to medium and coat with cooking spray.

Dip bread in egg mixture, then coat with the cereal mixture.

Cook on the griddle for about 3 mins on each side.

Serve topped with maple syrup.

Nutrition Facts (1 portion):

Energy: 335 Kcal

Carbs: 43g

Proteins: 17g

Fats: 11g

Sweet Potato and Egg Skillet

Portion Size: 2

Duration: 25 min

Ingredients:

1 Tbsp Butter

1 medium Sweet Potato, peeled and sliced

1/2 Garlic clove, chopped

Salt and Dry Thyme to taste

1 cup Fresh Baby Spinach

2 Large Eggs

1/4 tsp Ground Pepper

Instructions:

Melt butter on the Blackstone Griddle over medium heat.

Cook sweet potatoes covered for about 5 mins until almost done.

Add garlic, thyme, and spinach. Cook for 2 more minutes.

Make four wells in the potato mixture and crack an egg into each.

Season with salt and pepper. Cook covered until eggs are set to your liking.

Nutrition Facts (1 portion):

Energy: 224 Kcal

Carbs: 24g

Proteins: 8g

Fats: 11g

Waffle Breakfast Sandwich

Portion Size: 2

Duration: 12 minutes

Ingredients:

1 Waffle, halved

1 Egg, scrambled

1/2 slice of Cheese

1 slice Ham (or any lunch meat)

Instructions:

Preheat the Blackstone Griddle to medium heat.

Place halved waffles on the griddle and cook for about 5 minutes until lightly toasted.

Add scrambled egg on top of each waffle half.

Top with cheese and a slice of ham.

Serve warm with optional butter syrup drizzled on top.

Nutrition Facts (1 portion):

Energy: 25 Kcal

Carbs: 0.26g

Proteins: 1.6g

Fats: 1.94g

Griddle Pancakes with Caramelized Bananas

Portion Size: 2

Duration: 20 min

Ingredients:

1 cup all-purpose flour

1 tbsp sugar

1 tsp baking powder

1/2 tsp baking soda

1/4 tsp salt

1 cup buttermilk

1 egg

2 tbsp melted butter

2 bananas, sliced

2 tbsp brown sugar

Maple syrup for serving

Instructions:

In a bowl, mix flour, sugar, baking powder, baking soda, and salt.

In another bowl, whisk together buttermilk, egg, and melted butter.

Combine the wet ingredients with the dry ingredients until just mixed.

Preheat the Blackstone griddle to medium heat and grease with butter or oil.

Pour 1/4 cup of batter for each pancake and cook until bubbles form on the surface. Flip and cook until golden brown.

For the caramelized bananas, sprinkle brown sugar over the banana slices and cook on the griddle until caramelized.

Serve the pancakes topped with caramelized bananas and maple syrup.

Nutrition Facts (1 portion):

Energy: 520 Kcal

Carbs: 82g

Proteins: 15g

Fats: 16g

Potato Frittata

Portion Size: 2

Duration: 20 min

Ingredients:

1 Tbsp Olive Oil

1 cup Yellow Onions, chopped

1/2 lb Baking Potatoes, diced

Salt and Pepper to taste

1.5 Tbsp Butter

4 large Eggs, lightly whisked

1 Tbsp Chives, chopped

1/2 Tbsp Cilantro, chopped

1/4 of an 8-oz pack Shredded Pizza Cheese

1/4 cup Salsa, warmed

Instructions:

Heat oil on the Blackstone Griddle over medium heat.

Add onions and cook for 2-3 minutes.

Add potatoes and cook for 10 minutes until golden.

Season with salt and pepper. Add butter and eggs.

Cook, stirring occasionally, for 2-3 minutes until nearly set.

Sprinkle with cilantro and chives.

Spread evenly and top with cheese.

Serve in wedges with salsa.

Nutrition Facts (1 portion):

Energy: 480 Kcal

Carbs: 30g

Proteins: 22g

Fats: 29g

Mango on Multigrain Toast

Portion Size: 2
Duration: 10 min

Ingredients:

1/2 Mango, sliced

1/2 Tbsp Maple Syrup

2 slices Multigrain Bread, toasted

2 oz Camembert Cheese, sliced

Pepper to taste

Instructions:

Combine mango and syrup in a small bowl.

Place a slice of cheese on each toast.

Top with 1/4 of the mango mixture and a sprinkle of pepper.

Nutrition Facts (1 portion):

Energy: 280 Kcal

Carbs: 43g

Proteins: 10g

Fats: 7g

Breakfast Burritos

Portion Size: 2
Duration: 10 min

Ingredients:

2 Large Eggs

2 Gordita Style Fajita Tortillas (8-inch)

1/4 of a 5-oz pack Baby Spinach

1/4 cup Mexican Shredded Cheese

Cooking Spray

2 Tbsp Mild Salsa

Instructions:

Whisk eggs in a bowl. Set aside.

Preheat the Blackstone Griddle to medium-high.

Heat tortillas on the griddle for 15 seconds each side. Keep warm.

Spray the griddle with cooking spray.

Add eggs, cheese, and spinach. Cook, stirring frequently, for 1-1 1/2 minutes.

Season with salt and pepper.

Divide egg mixture onto the center of each tortilla.

Add 1 Tbsp salsa to each.

Fold and roll into burritos.

Nutrition Facts (1 portion):

Energy: 270 Kcal

Carbs: 28g

Proteins: 14g

Fats: 12g

Egg & Cheese Bagel Sandwich

Portion Size: 2
Duration: 15 minutes

Ingredients:
2 Plain Bagels
Olive Oil Cooking Spray
2 Large Eggs
Salt and Pepper to taste
2 slices Yellow American Cheese

Instructions:
Preheat the Blackstone Griddle to medium heat and lightly spray with olive oil cooking spray.

Crack eggs onto the griddle and season with salt and pepper.

Cook the eggs for 3-4 minutes, or until the yolks are cooked to your desired doneness.

Place a slice of cheese on each egg during the last minute of cooking.

Toast the bagels on the griddle until lightly browned.

Assemble the sandwich with the cheese-topped egg on the toasted bagel bottom.

Serve immediately.

Nutrition Facts (1 portion):
Energy: 420 Kcal
Carbs: 64g
Proteins: 19g
Fats: 11g

Smoked Salmon and Cream Cheese Bagels

Portion Size: 2
Duration: 10 min

Ingredients:
2 bagels, halved
4 oz smoked salmon
4 tbsp cream cheese
1/2 red onion, thinly sliced
1 tbsp capers
Fresh dill for garnish
Lemon wedges for serving

Instructions:
Preheat the Blackstone griddle to a medium setting.

Lightly toast the bagel halves on the griddle until golden brown.

Spread cream cheese on each bagel half.

Top with smoked salmon, red onion slices, capers, and fresh dill.

Serve with a wedge of lemon on the side.

Nutrition Facts (1 portion):
Energy: 390 Kcal
Carbs: 48g
Proteins: 22g
Fats: 12g

Avocado Toast with Soft-Boiled Egg

Portion Size: 2
Duration: 15 min

Ingredients:
2 slices Sprouted Multigrain Sandwich Bread
1 Avocado, smashed
2 Large Brown Eggs, soft-boiled and sliced
Hot Habanero Pepper Sauce to taste
Salt and Pepper to taste

Instructions:
Toast the bread slices on the griddle until golden brown.

Spread smashed avocado evenly on each slice of toast.

Top with sliced soft-boiled eggs.

Season with salt, pepper, and hot sauce to taste.

Nutrition Facts (1 portion):

Energy: 330 Kcal

Carbs: 26g

Proteins: 12g

Fats: 20g

Appetizers and Side Dishes

Fats: 42g

Griddle Breakfast Skillet

Portion Size: 2
Duration: 30 min

Ingredients:
1/2 lb diced potatoes
1/2 lb breakfast sausage, crumbled
1/2 bell pepper, diced
1/2 onion, diced
4 eggs
1/2 cup shredded cheddar cheese
2 tbsp olive oil
Salt and pepper to taste
Chopped green onions for garnish

Instructions:
Preheat the Blackstone griddle to medium heat.

Add olive oil and potatoes to the griddle. Cook until they start to brown.

Add the breakfast sausage, bell pepper, and onion. Cook until the sausage is browned and the vegetables are soft.

Make four wells in the mixture and crack an egg into each.

Sprinkle salt and pepper over the eggs and cook until they reach your desired doneness.

Sprinkle cheddar cheese over the top and let it melt.

Garnish with chopped green onions.
Serve hot directly from the griddle.

Nutrition Facts (1 portion):
Energy: 650 Kcal
Carbs: 38g
Proteins: 28g

Grilled Veggie Skewers

Portion Size: 2
Duration: 20 minutes

Ingredients:
1/2 zucchini, cut into chunks
1/2 yellow squash, cut into chunks
1/2 red bell pepper, cut into chunks
1/2 onion, cut into chunks
1 tbsp olive oil
Salt and pepper, to taste
1 tsp dried Italian herbs

Instructions:
Preheat the Blackstone Griddle to medium-high heat.

Thread the zucchini, yellow squash, bell pepper, and onion onto skewers.

Brush the vegetables with olive oil and season with salt, pepper, and Italian herbs.

Grill the skewers on the griddle, turning occasionally, for about 10-15 minutes or until vegetables are tender and slightly charred.

Serve warm as a side dish or appetizer.

Nutrition Facts (1 portion):
Energy: 120 Kcal
Carbs: 10g
Proteins: 2g
Fats: 9g

Griddle-Seared Green Beans

Portion Size: 2
Duration: 12 minutes

Ingredients:

2 cups fresh green beans, trimmed

1 tbsp olive oil

1 garlic clove, minced

Salt and pepper, to taste

1/4 tsp red pepper flakes

Lemon zest (optional)

Instructions:

Preheat your Blackstone Griddle to medium heat.

Toss green beans with olive oil, garlic, salt, pepper, and red pepper flakes.

Spread the green beans on the griddle and cook for about 10 minutes, stirring occasionally, until they are tender and slightly charred.

Garnish with lemon zest for added flavor.

Nutrition Facts (1 portion):

Energy: 70 Kcal

Carbs: 8g

Proteins: 2g

Fats: 4g

Grilled Bruschetta

Portion Size: 2
Duration: 15 minutes

Ingredients:

4 slices of rustic bread

1/2 cup cherry tomatoes, halved

1/4 cup fresh basil, chopped

1 garlic clove, minced

2 tbsp olive oil

Salt and pepper, to taste

Balsamic glaze (optional)

Instructions:

Preheat your Blackstone Griddle to medium-high heat.

In a bowl, mix together tomatoes, basil, garlic, 1 tbsp olive oil, salt, and pepper.

Brush the bread slices with the remaining olive oil.

Grill the bread on the griddle for about 2 minutes per side, until golden and crisp.

Top the grilled bread with the tomato mixture. Drizzle with balsamic glaze if desired.

Nutrition Facts (1 portion):

Energy: 180 Kcal

Carbs: 23g

Proteins: 4g

Fats: 8g

Griddle Garlic Bread

Portion Size: 2
Duration: 10 minutes

Ingredients:

2 slices of thick Italian bread

2 tbsp butter, softened

1 garlic clove, minced

1 tbsp grated Parmesan cheese

1 tsp chopped parsley

Instructions:

Preheat the Blackstone Griddle to medium heat.

Mix butter with minced garlic, Parmesan, and parsley in a small bowl.

Spread the garlic butter mixture on one side of each bread slice.

Place the bread, buttered side down, on the griddle.

Grill for about 5 minutes or until the bread is golden brown and crispy.

Flip and grill the other side for an additional 2 minutes.

Serve warm as an appetizer or side dish.

Nutrition Facts (1 portion):
Energy: 210 Kcal
Carbs: 22g
Proteins: 4g
Fats: 12g

Griddle Roasted Potatoes

Portion Size: 2
Duration: 30 minutes

Ingredients:
2 medium potatoes, sliced
1 tbsp olive oil
1/2 tsp smoked paprika
Salt and pepper, to taste
1/2 tsp garlic powder
1/2 tsp onion powder

Instructions:
Preheat the Blackstone Griddle to medium-high heat.

Toss the potato slices with olive oil, smoked paprika, garlic powder, onion powder, salt, and pepper.

Arrange the potatoes on the griddle in a single layer.

Cook for about 15 minutes, turning occasionally, until the potatoes are golden brown and tender.

Serve as a delicious side dish.

Nutrition Facts (1 portion):
Energy: 190 Kcal
Carbs: 28g
Proteins: 3g
Fats: 7g

Quinoa with Peas and Onion

Portion Size: 2
Duration: 30 min

Ingredients:
3/4 cup Water
1/3 cup Quinoa, rinsed
1/3 Small Onion, sliced
1/2 Tbsp Olive Oil
1/3 cup Frozen Peas
A pinch of Salt and Pepper
1/3 Tbsp Walnuts, chopped

Instructions:
Boil water in a pot on the griddle. Add quinoa, cover, and cook for 12 minutes.

In a separate pan on the griddle, sauté onion in olive oil until tender.

Mix cooked quinoa with onions.

Add peas, salt, and pepper. Heat through.

Sprinkle with chopped walnuts.

Nutrition Facts (1 portion):
Energy: 171 Kcal
Carbs: 24.19g
Proteins: 6g
Fats: 5.57g

Sweet Corn Dish

Portion Size: 2
Duration: 22 minutes

Ingredients:
3 oz Creamed Corn
1/4 cup Desiccated Coconut
1/2 Egg, slightly beaten
1/2 Tomato, sliced

Instructions:
Preheat the Blackstone Griddle to a medium setting.
In a bowl, mix together creamed corn, coconut, and egg.
Transfer the mixture into a griddle-safe dish.
Top with sliced tomato.
Cook on the griddle for about 20 minutes, or until set.

Nutrition Facts (1 portion):
Energy: 237 Kcal
Carbs: 23.24g
Proteins: 4.56g
Fats: 15.5g

Crispy Baked Onion Rings

Portion Size: 2
Duration: 30 minutes

Ingredients:
1/2 lb Sweet Onions, cut into 1/2-inch rings
1 1/2 Egg Whites
1/2 cup Dry Breadcrumbs
1 tsp Thyme Powder
1/2 tsp Paprika
1 tsp Salt
1/8 tsp Pepper

Instructions:
Soak onion rings in an ice bath for 30 minutes, then drain.
Beat egg whites until foamy.
In a bowl, mix breadcrumbs, thyme, paprika, salt, and pepper.
Dip onion rings in egg whites, then coat in breadcrumbs.
Cook on the griddle for about 20 minutes, flipping halfway, until crisp and lightly browned.

Nutrition Facts (1 portion):
Energy: 159 Kcal
Carbs: 29g
Proteins: 7g
Fats: 2g

Grilled Corn on the Cob

Portion Size: 2
Duration: 15 minutes

Ingredients:
2 Ears of Corn, shucked
1 Tbsp Basting Oil
Salt, to taste

Instructions:
Preheat the Blackstone Griddle to medium-high heat.
Brush corn with basting oil.
Place corn on the griddle, turning frequently, and grill for 8-10 minutes.
Season with salt and serve.

Nutrition Facts (1 portion):
Energy: 150 Kcal

Carbs: 19g

Proteins: 3g

Fats: 8g

Glazed Sweet Potatoes

Portion Size*: 2*

Duration*: 60 minutes*

Ingredients*:*

1/2 lb Sweet Potatoes

1/10 cup Butter, cubed

1/10 cup Maple Syrup

2 tbsp Brown Sugar

1/10 tsp Ground Cinnamon

Instructions*:*

Boil sweet potatoes until tender, about 35 minutes. Cool, peel, and slice.

Preheat the griddle to 350°F.

In a small pot on the griddle, combine butter, syrup, sugar, and cinnamon. Boil and stir.

Pour over sliced potatoes.

Cook for 30-40 minutes, until glazed.

Nutrition Facts (1 portion):

Energy: 200 Kcal

Carbs: 36g

Proteins: 2.34g

Fats: 5.75g

Griddle-Roasted Peppers and Onions

Portion Size*: 2*

Duration*: 15 minutes*

Ingredients*:*

1 red bell pepper, sliced

1 green bell pepper, sliced

1 yellow bell pepper, sliced

1 medium onion, sliced

2 tbsp olive oil

1/2 tsp smoked paprika

Salt and pepper, to taste

Instructions*:*

Preheat the Blackstone Griddle to medium heat.

In a large bowl, toss the sliced peppers and onions with olive oil, smoked paprika, salt, and pepper.

Spread the vegetables evenly on the griddle.

Cook for about 10-12 minutes, stirring occasionally, until the vegetables are tender and have a nice char.

Serve as a colorful and flavorful side dish or topping for grilled meats.

Nutrition Facts (1 portion):

Energy: 110 Kcal

Carbs: 10g

Proteins: 2g

Fats: 7g

Grilled Shrimp Skewers

Portion Size*: 2*

Duration*: 15 minutes*

Ingredients*:*

12 large shrimp, peeled and deveined

1 tbsp olive oil

1 tsp lemon zest

1 garlic clove, minced

1/2 tsp paprika

Salt and pepper, to taste

Lemon wedges, for serving

Instructions:

Preheat the Blackstone Griddle to medium-high heat.

In a bowl, mix olive oil, lemon zest, minced garlic, paprika, salt, and pepper.

Toss the shrimp in the marinade and let sit for 5 minutes.

Thread the shrimp onto skewers.

Grill the skewers on the griddle for about 2-3 minutes per side, or until the shrimp are pink and cooked through.

Serve with lemon wedges.

Nutrition Facts (1 portion):

Energy: 120 Kcal

Carbs: 1g

Proteins: 23g

Fats: 3g

Griddle Asparagus with Parmesan

Portion Size: 2

Duration: 10 minutes

Ingredients:

1 bunch of asparagus, trimmed

1 tbsp olive oil

Salt and pepper, to taste

2 tbsp grated Parmesan cheese

1/2 lemon, for juice

Instructions:

Preheat the Blackstone Griddle to medium heat.

Toss the asparagus with olive oil, salt, and pepper.

Place the asparagus on the griddle and cook for about 5-7 minutes, turning occasionally, until they are tender and slightly charred.

Squeeze lemon juice over the asparagus and sprinkle with grated Parmesan cheese.

Serve immediately.

Nutrition Facts (1 portion):

Energy: 80 Kcal

Carbs: 4g

Proteins: 5g

Fats: 6g

Grilled Peach Salsa

Portion Size: 2

Duration: 30 min

Ingredients:

1 Peach, halved

1 cup Salsa Verde

Juice and Zest of 1 Lime

1 Avocado, diced

2 tsp Cilantro, chopped

Salt and Pepper to taste

Instructions:

Preheat the Blackstone Griddle to high heat.

Grill the peach halves cut side down for 3-4 minutes until slightly browned.

Dice the grilled peach and mix with salsa, lime juice, avocado, and cilantro.

Season with salt and pepper as desired.

Nutrition Facts (1 portion):

Energy: 20 Kcal

Carbs: 2g

Proteins: 0g

Fats: 2g

Asian Cucumbers

Portion Size: 2
Duration: 1 hour 10 min

Ingredients:
1 cup Seasoned Rice Vinegar
1 Organic Seedless Cucumber, thinly sliced
1 Shallot, thinly sliced

Instructions:
Bring rice vinegar to a boil on the griddle over medium-high heat.

Mix in shallots and cucumbers.

Let sit at room temperature for an hour, then serve chilled.

Nutrition Facts (1 portion):
Energy: 25 Kcal
Carbs: 6g
Proteins: 1g
Fats: 0g

Grilled Cauliflower Wedges

Portion Size: 2
Duration: 35 min

Ingredients:
1/3 Cauliflower, cut into wedges
1/6 cup Salted Peanuts
1/6 cup Strong Cheddar Cheese, shredded
1/6 cup Chicken Broth, spiced

Instructions:
Spread cauliflower wedges on a large piece of foil.

Sprinkle with peanuts, cheese, and chicken broth.

Seal the foil packet and place on the Blackstone Griddle over medium heat.

Grill for 20-25 minutes, turning occasionally.

Nutrition Facts (1 portion):
Energy: 103 Kcal
Carbs: 6g
Proteins: 6g
Fats: 7g

Chicken Dijon

Portion Size: 2
Duration: 30 min

Ingredients:
3 Tbsp Butter
2 Chicken Breasts, skin and bones
14 oz Chicken Broth
1 Medium Onion, chopped
3 Tbsp All-Purpose Flour
3 Tbsp Dijon Mustard

Instructions:
Melt butter on the griddle over medium-high heat. Cook chicken until golden brown on both sides.

In a separate bowl, whisk together broth, onion, flour, and mustard.

Pour mixture over chicken and simmer for 20 minutes on low heat.

Nutrition Facts (1 portion):
Energy: 528 Kcal
Carbs: 46.5g
Proteins: 7.88g
Fats: 36.5g

Brussels Sprouts with Pecans

Portion Size*:* 2
Duration*:* 10 min

Ingredients*:*
1/3 lb Brussels Sprouts, halved
1/6 lb Pecans, halves
2 tsp Butter
Salt and Pepper to taste

Instructions*:*
Sauté brussels sprouts and pecans in butter on the griddle for 5-7 minutes until crisp-tender. Season with salt and pepper.

Nutrition Facts (1 portion):
Energy: 335 Kcal
Carbs: 12.15g
Proteins: 6.1g
Fats: 31.8g

Griddled Halloumi and Tomato Skewers

Portion Size*:* 2
Duration*:* 10 minutes

Ingredients*:*
1/2 block halloumi cheese, cut into cubes
8 cherry tomatoes
1 tbsp olive oil
1 tsp dried oregano
Salt and pepper, to taste

Instructions*:*
Preheat the Blackstone Griddle to medium-high heat.

Thread halloumi cubes and cherry tomatoes alternately onto skewers.

Brush the skewers with olive oil and season with oregano, salt, and pepper.

Grill on the griddle for about 2-3 minutes per side, or until the halloumi is golden and the tomatoes are slightly charred.

Serve immediately as a flavorful appetizer or side.

Nutrition Facts (1 portion):
Energy: 180 Kcal
Carbs: 4g
Proteins: 12g
Fats: 14g

Flavorful Green Rice

Portion Size*:* 2
Duration*:* 30 min

Ingredients*:*
1/4 cup Green Onions, finely sliced
2 1/2 tsp Olive Oil
1/8 cup Parsley, finely chopped
2 1/2 tsp Butter
1/3 cup Rice, uncooked
1/9 cup Chicken Broth
1/10 tsp Cayenne Pepper
1 Bay Leaf

Instructions*:*
Sauté onions and parsley in oil and butter on the griddle for 1 minute.

Add rice and cook until transparent.

Stir in broth, cayenne pepper, and bay leaf. Bring to a boil, then simmer covered for 18-20 minutes.

Remove the bay leaf before serving.

Nutrition Facts (1 portion):

Energy: 240 Kcal

Carbs: 39g

Proteins: 5g

Fats: 7g

Salads and vegetarian dishes

Grilled Vegetable Salad with Feta Cheese

Portion Size: 2
Duration: 20 min

Ingredients:

1 zucchini, sliced lengthwise

1 red bell pepper, sliced into strips

1 yellow bell pepper, sliced into strips

1/2 eggplant, sliced

2 tbsp olive oil

Salt and pepper, to taste

1/4 cup feta cheese, crumbled

2 tbsp balsamic vinegar

1 tbsp fresh basil, chopped

Instructions:

Preheat your Blackstone Griddle to medium-high heat.

Brush the zucchini, bell peppers, and eggplant with olive oil, and season with salt and pepper.

Grill the vegetables on the griddle, turning occasionally, until they are tender and have grill marks, about 10-15 minutes.

Transfer the grilled vegetables to a serving plate.

Sprinkle with feta cheese, drizzle with balsamic vinegar, and garnish with fresh basil.

Serve the salad warm or at room temperature.

Nutrition Facts (1 portion):

Energy: 250 Kcal

Carbs: 18g

Proteins: 7g

Fats: 17g

Vegetable Korma Recipe

Portion Size: 2
Duration: 25 min

Ingredients:

1 Tbsp Vegetable Oil

1/2 Red Onion, wedged

1 Carrot, thickly sliced

1/2 Cauliflower, florets

1/2 Green Chili Pepper, chopped

1 Garlic Clove, crushed

1/2 Tbsp Ginger, chopped

1/2 tsp Cumin Powder

A pinch of Coriander Powder

1/2 tsp Garam Masala

1/3 cup Vegetable Stock

Salt to taste

1 1/2 oz Frozen Peas

3 tbsp Natural Yogurt

Instructions:

On the griddle, heat oil in a pan over medium heat and add onion. Cook for 3-4 minutes.

Add carrots, cauliflower, chili, garlic, ginger, and spices. Cook for 3 minutes.

Pour in the stock, cover, and cook for 6-7 minutes.

Add peas and cook for 2-3 minutes.

Turn off heat and stir in yogurt. Serve with rice.

Nutrition Facts (1 portion):

Energy: 301 Kcal

Carbs: 46g

Proteins: 5g

Fats: 7g

Chickpea and Spinach Griddle Tacos

Portion Size: 2
Duration: 15 min

Ingredients:

1 cup cooked chickpeas, drained

2 cups baby spinach

1 garlic clove, minced

1/2 tsp cumin

Salt and pepper, to taste

4 small corn tortillas

1/4 cup salsa

1/4 cup shredded cheddar cheese

Instructions:

Preheat your Blackstone Griddle to medium heat.

Add chickpeas, garlic, cumin, salt, and pepper to the griddle. Cook for 5 minutes, stirring occasionally.

Add spinach and cook until wilted, about 2 minutes.

Warm tortillas on the griddle for about 30 seconds on each side.

Assemble the tacos by placing the chickpea and spinach mixture onto tortillas, topping with salsa and cheese.

Serve immediately.

Nutrition Facts (1 portion):

Energy: 215 Kcal

Carbs: 32g

Proteins: 10g

Fats: 7g

Lemony Chickpeas

Portion Size: 2

Duration: 30 min

Ingredients:

1 cup Instant Brown Rice, uncooked

1/2 cup Olive Oil

1 Medium Onion, chopped

1 can Chickpeas, drained

7 oz Canned Diced Tomatoes, undrained

1/2 cup Vegetable Broth

1/8 tsp Red Pepper Flakes

1 1/2 Tbsp Lemon Juice

1/4 tsp Lemon Zest

1/8 tsp Pepper

Instructions:

Prepare rice as per instructions.

On the griddle, heat oil in a skillet and cook onion until soft.

Add chickpeas, tomatoes, broth, pepper, and red pepper flakes.

Simmer covered for 10 minutes.

Uncover and cook until liquid reduces.

Stir in lemon juice and zest. Serve with rice.

Nutrition Facts (1 portion):

Energy: 433 Kcal

Carbs: 76g

Proteins: 13g

Fats: 9g

Rainbow Hash

Portion Size: 2
Duration: 30 min

Ingredients:

2 Tbsp Coconut or Olive Oil

1 Medium Purple Potato, diced

1/2 tsp Dried Oregano

1/2 tsp Pepper

1/2 tsp Dried Basil

1/2 tsp Sea Salt

2 cups Kale or Spinach, chopped

1 Large Carrot, diced

1 Garlic Clove

Instructions:

Heat oil on the griddle at medium temperature.

Cook potatoes, carrot, and seasonings for 10-12 minutes until soft.

Add kale and garlic, cook for 2-4 minutes.

Nutrition Facts (1 portion):

Energy: 304 Kcal

Carbs: 43g

Proteins: 4g

Fats: 14g

Warm Cabbage, Fennel, and Pear Salad

Portion Size: 2

Duration: 25 min

Ingredients:

1 Medium Pear

1 tbsp Lemon Juice

1 1/2 Tbsp Olive Oil

1/2 Fennel Bulb, sliced

2 cups Cabbage, shredded

1/8 cup Water

1 Tbsp Lemon Juice

1 tsp Agave Nectar

1/2 tsp Kosher Salt

1/2 tsp Pepper

1/2 cup Gorgonzola Cheese, crumbled

1/4 cup Walnuts, toasted

Instructions:

Peel and core pear, then slice.

Toss pear slices with 1 tbsp lemon juice.

Heat oil on the griddle and cook fennel until crisp-tender.

Add cabbage, cook until soft.

Add pears, water, agave, lemon juice, salt, and pepper.

Cook until liquid evaporates.

Serve topped with Gorgonzola and walnuts.

Nutrition Facts (1 portion):

Energy: 391 Kcal

Carbs: 28g

Proteins: 9g

Fats: 26g

Arugula & Brown Rice Salad

Portion Size: 2

Duration: 25 min

Ingredients:

8.8 oz Brown Rice, prepared

3 cups Arugula or Spinach

1/2 can Chickpeas, rinsed

1/2 cup Feta Cheese, crumbled

1/2 cup Basil Leaves, torn

1/4 cup Dried Cranberries or Cherries

Dressing:

1/8 cup Olive Oil

1 Tbsp Lemon Juice

1/8 tsp Lemon Zest

1/8 tsp Salt and Pepper each

Instructions:

Heat rice as directed and let it cool slightly.

Mix rice with arugula, chickpeas, cheese, basil, and cranberries.

Combine dressing ingredients and drizzle over the salad.

Toss to coat and serve.

Nutrition Facts (1 portion):
Energy: 236 Kcal

Carbs: 26g

Proteins: 6g

Fats: 11g

Ginger-Kale Smoothies

Portion Size: 2

Duration: 15 min

Ingredients:
1 cup Orange Juice

2 cups Kale, torn

1/8 tsp Turmeric Powder

4 Ice Cubes

1 tbsp Ginger Root, fresh, chopped

1 tsp Lemon Juice

1/8 tsp Cinnamon Powder

Dash of Cayenne Pepper

1 medium Apple, peeled, chopped

Chopped Turmeric, optional

Instructions:
Blend all **ingredients** until smooth.

Pour into chilled glasses and serve immediately.

Nutrition Facts (1 portion):
Energy: 121 Kcal

Carbs: 29g

Proteins: 1g

Fats: 0g

Grilled Portobello Mushroom Steaks

Portion Size: 2

Duration: 25 min

Ingredients:
2 large portobello mushrooms, stems removed

3 tbsp soy sauce

2 tbsp olive oil

1 tbsp balsamic vinegar

1 garlic clove, minced

1 tsp smoked paprika

Salt and pepper, to taste

Instructions:
In a small bowl, whisk together soy sauce, olive oil, balsamic vinegar, garlic, smoked paprika, salt, and pepper.

Brush the portobello mushrooms with the marinade and let them sit for 10 minutes.

Preheat your Blackstone Griddle to medium-high heat.

Place the mushrooms on the griddle, gill-side up, and cook for 5 minutes. Flip and cook for another 5 minutes.

Serve the grilled portobello mushrooms as a vegetarian steak alternative.

Nutrition Facts (1 portion):
Energy: 190 Kcal

Carbs: 10g

Proteins: 6g

Fats: 14g

Avocado and Tomato Griddle Salad

Portion Size: 2

Duration: 10 min

Ingredients:

2 ripe avocados, sliced

1 cup cherry tomatoes, halved

1/4 red onion, thinly sliced

2 tbsp olive oil

Juice of 1 lime

Salt and pepper, to taste

2 tbsp fresh cilantro, chopped

Instructions:

Preheat your Blackstone Griddle to medium heat.

Lightly brush the avocado slices with olive oil and place them on the griddle. Grill for about 2 minutes on each side, until they have nice grill marks.

In a salad bowl, combine grilled avocados, cherry tomatoes, and red onion.

Drizzle with the remaining olive oil and lime juice. Season with salt and pepper.

Garnish with fresh cilantro and serve immediately.

Nutrition Facts (1 portion):

Energy: 320 Kcal

Carbs: 20g

Proteins: 4g

Fats: 27g

Griddled Bell Peppers with Feta and Pine Nuts

Portion Size: 2
Duration: 15 min

Ingredients:

2 bell peppers, assorted colors, sliced

1 tbsp olive oil

Salt and pepper, to taste

1/4 cup feta cheese, crumbled

2 tbsp pine nuts, toasted

1 tbsp balsamic reduction

Instructions:

Preheat your Blackstone Griddle to medium-high heat.

Toss bell pepper slices with olive oil, salt, and pepper.

Grill the pepper slices on the griddle for about 5-7 minutes, turning occasionally, until they are tender and charred.

Arrange grilled peppers on a serving plate.

Sprinkle with crumbled feta cheese and toasted pine nuts.

Drizzle with balsamic reduction and serve.

Nutrition Facts (1 portion):

Energy: 210 Kcal

Carbs: 12g

Proteins: 5g

Fats: 16g

Spiced Grilled Eggplant Rounds

Portion Size: 2
Duration: 20 min

Ingredients:

1 large eggplant, sliced into rounds

2 tbsp olive oil

1/2 tsp ground cumin

1/2 tsp paprika

Salt and pepper, to taste

2 tbsp fresh parsley, chopped

1/4 cup yogurt, for serving (optional)

Instructions:

In a small bowl, mix together olive oil, cumin, paprika, salt, and pepper.

Brush both sides of the eggplant slices with the spiced oil mixture.

Preheat your Blackstone Griddle to medium heat.

Grill the eggplant rounds for about 4-5 minutes on each side, until tender and nicely charred.

Transfer to a serving plate and sprinkle with chopped parsley.

Serve with a dollop of yogurt on the side, if desired.

Nutrition Facts (1 portion):

Energy: 180 Kcal

Carbs: 15g

Proteins: 3g

Fats: 13g

Zucchini and Corn Griddle Cakes

Portion Size: 2

Duration: 20 min

Ingredients:

1 large zucchini, grated

1/2 cup sweet corn kernels

1/4 cup flour

1 egg, beaten

1/4 cup green onions, chopped

1/2 tsp garlic powder

Salt and pepper, to taste

2 tbsp vegetable oil

Instructions:

Combine grated zucchini, corn, flour, beaten egg, green onions, garlic powder, salt, and pepper in a bowl. Mix well.

Heat vegetable oil on the Blackstone Griddle over medium heat.

Scoop spoonfuls of the zucchini mixture onto the griddle. Flatten to form cakes.

Cook for about 4-5 minutes per side or until golden and crispy.

Serve hot, perhaps with a dollop of sour cream or yogurt.

Nutrition Facts (1 portion):

Energy: 225 Kcal

Carbs: 27g

Proteins: 6g

Fats: 10g

Griddled Asparagus with Lemon Butter

Portion Size: 2

Duration: 15 min

Ingredients:

1 bunch asparagus, trimmed

2 tbsp butter, melted

1 tsp lemon zest

Juice of 1/2 lemon

Salt and pepper, to taste

Parmesan cheese, grated (optional)

Instructions:

Toss asparagus with melted butter, lemon zest, lemon juice, salt, and pepper.

Preheat Blackstone Griddle to medium heat.

Place asparagus on the griddle and cook for about 6-8 minutes, turning occasionally, until tender and lightly charred.

Transfer to a serving dish and, if desired, sprinkle with grated Parmesan cheese.

Serve immediately.

Nutrition Facts (1 portion):
Energy: 90 Kcal
Carbs: 4g
Proteins: 3g
Fats: 7g

Mushroom & Zucchini Pesto Sauté

Portion Size: 2
Duration: 10 min

Ingredients:
1 tsp Olive Oil
1/4 lb Fresh Mushrooms, sliced
1/2 Small Onion, chopped
1 Medium Zucchini, sliced
1 1/2 Tbsp Prepared Pesto
1/8 tsp Lemon-Pepper Seasoning

Instructions:
Heat olive oil on the griddle.
Sauté onion and mushrooms for 2 minutes.
Add zucchini and cook until soft.
Stir in pesto and lemon-pepper seasoning.

Nutrition Facts (1 portion):
Energy: 99 Kcal
Carbs: 8g
Proteins: 4g
Fats: 7g

Crispy Tofu and Veggie Stir-Fry

Portion Size: 2
Duration: 25 min

Ingredients:
1/2 block firm tofu, pressed and cubed
1 cup mixed bell peppers, sliced
1/2 cup snap peas
1 carrot, sliced
2 tbsp soy sauce
1 tbsp honey or maple syrup
1 garlic clove, minced
1 tsp ginger, grated
2 tbsp vegetable oil
Sesame seeds for garnish

Instructions:
In a bowl, mix soy sauce, honey/maple syrup, garlic, and ginger. Set aside.

Heat 1 tbsp oil on the Blackstone Griddle over medium-high heat. Add tofu and cook until all sides are golden and crispy. Remove and set aside.

Add the remaining oil to the griddle. Stir-fry bell peppers, snap peas, and carrot until tender-crisp.

Return tofu to the griddle, add the sauce, and toss everything together.

Garnish with sesame seeds and serve immediately.

Nutrition Facts (1 portion):
Energy: 215 Kcal
Carbs: 18g
Proteins: 10g
Fats: 12g

Apple-White Cheddar Grilled Cheese

Portion Size*: 2*
Duration*: 20 min*

Ingredients*:*

3 oz Cheddar Cheese

1 Thin Red Onion Slice, separated into rings

4 Slices Whole Wheat Cinnamon-Raisin Bread

1/4 tsp Red Pepper Flakes (optional)

1 Small Apple, thinly sliced

1 Tbsp Butter, softened

Instructions*:*

Place cheese, apple, and onion on two bread slices.

Sprinkle with red pepper flakes if desired.

Top with remaining bread.

Butter the outside of the sandwiches.

Grill on the griddle until golden brown.

Nutrition Facts (1 portion):

Energy: 456 Kcal

Carbs: 37g

Proteins: 20g

Fats: 27g

Zucchini Pancakes

Portion Size*: 2*
Duration*: 20 min*

Ingredients*:*

1 1/2 cups Grated Zucchini

3 tbsp Parmesan Cheese, finely grated

1 Large Egg, beaten with a dash of pepper

1 Tbsp Canola Oil

2 Tbsp Biscuit/Baking Mix

Sour Cream (optional)

Instructions*:*

Squeeze and drain zucchini.

Mix egg, cheese, baking mix, and pepper in a bowl. Stir in zucchini.

Heat oil on the griddle over medium heat.

Drop pancake batter and flatten slightly.

Cook each side for about 2 minutes. Serve with sour cream if desired.

Nutrition Facts (1 portion):

Energy: 174 Kcal

Carbs: 9g

Proteins: 7g

Fats: 13g

Grilled Mixed Fruit & Vegetable Kabobs

Portion Size*: 2*
Duration*: 20 min*

Ingredients*:*

1/2 Bell Pepper, diced

6 Pineapple Chunks

1/2 Zucchini, cut

1 Tbsp Basting Oil

1/2 Sweet Onion, quartered

1/2 Tbsp Balsamic Vinegar

Salt and Pepper to taste

Instructions*:*

Preheat the griddle.

Mix basting oil and vinegar in a bowl.

Thread veggies and pineapple onto skewers.

Brush with oil and vinegar mix.

Grill for 10 minutes, flipping occasionally.

Season with salt and pepper.

Nutrition Facts (1 portion):

Energy: 120 Kcal

Carbs: 17g

Proteins: 2g

Fats: 6g

Fats: 4g

Griddled Bell Pepper and Corn Salsa

Portion Size*: 2* ***Duration****: 20 min*

Ingredients*:*

1 red bell pepper, diced

1 cup corn kernels, fresh or frozen

1/4 red onion, finely chopped

1 jalapeño, seeded and minced

Juice of 1 lime

2 tbsp cilantro, chopped

Salt and pepper, to taste

1 tbsp olive oil

Instructions*:*

Preheat Blackstone Griddle to medium-high heat.

Toss bell pepper and corn with olive oil, and griddle for about 8-10 minutes, until charred and tender.

Remove from the griddle and let cool.

In a bowl, mix the grilled bell pepper and corn with red onion, jalapeño, lime juice, and cilantro.

Season with salt and pepper to taste.

Serve as a side or with chips.

Nutrition Facts (1 portion):

Energy: 120 Kcal

Carbs: 20g

Proteins: 3g

Fish and Seafood

Fish Dreams Recipe

Portion Size: 2
Duration: 45 min

Ingredients:
1 lb. Fish
1 Egg
1/8 tsp Paprika
1 Tbsp Flour
A pinch of Salt

Instructions:
Simmer fish in a small amount of water on the griddle for 5 minutes until it flakes easily. Drain and cool.

Separate egg whites and yolks. Beat yolks and mix with flour, paprika, and salt.

Flake fish and mix with egg yolk mixture.

Beat egg whites to peaks and fold into fish mixture.

Fry in hot oil on the griddle until golden brown on both sides.

Nutrition Facts (1 portion):
Energy: 719 Kcal
Carbs: 25g
Proteins: 55g
Fats: 44g

Fish Stock Recipe

Portion Size: 2
Duration: 21 min

Ingredients:
8 4/5 oz Fish Scraps
A pinch of Salt
1/4 tsp Cracked Pepper
1 tsp Lemon Juice
1/2 Bay Leaf
1/6 large Onion, chopped
1/2 medium Carrot, chopped
1/10 cup White Wine

Instructions:
Place fish scraps in a pot, cover with water, and boil on the griddle.

Simmer for 40 minutes. Remove fish flesh and refrigerate.

Simmer the stock again for 30 minutes.

Strain the stock and use as desired.

Nutrition Facts (1 portion):
Energy: 383 Kcal
Carbs: 15g
Proteins: 29g
Fats: 22g

Sea Scallops Sautéed with Mushrooms & Pasta

Portion Size: 2
Duration: 20 min

Ingredients:
2/3 lb. Sea Scallops, quartered
5 1/3 oz Pasta, cooked al dente
2 oz Mushrooms, sliced
2 tbsp Butter
2 Garlic cloves
1/4 cup White Wine
2/3 tsp Sea Salt
2 Tbsp Lemon Juice

Instructions:

Sauté scallops with garlic in butter on the griddle.

Remove scallops, leaving liquid. Add wine, lemon juice, and mushrooms. Sauté for 3 minutes.

Add cooked pasta and scallops back into the pan. Season with sea salt and lemon juice.

Cover, remove from heat, let sit for 5 minutes, then serve.

Nutrition Facts (1 portion):

Energy: 408 Kcal

Carbs: 30g

Proteins: 37g

Fats: 13g

Grilled Shrimp in the Shell

Portion Size: 2

Duration: 15 min

Ingredients:

1 lb. Fresh Wild Caught Shrimp

Salt and Pepper to taste

3 Tbsp Olive Oil

Instructions:

Preheat the griddle to HIGH.

Toss shrimp with salt, pepper, and olive oil.

Grill shrimp, covered, for 2-3 minutes on each side.

Remove from heat and let rest for 2 minutes.

Nutrition Facts (1 portion):

Energy: 190 Kcal

Carbs: 0g

Proteins: 36g

Fats: 5g

Grilled Scallop Kabob

Portion Size: 2

Duration: 30 min

Ingredients:

1/4 Yellow Bell Pepper, diced

1/4 Green Bell Pepper, diced

1/4 Orange Bell Pepper, diced

1/4 Red Onion, layered

10 Sea Scallops, Fresh

Instructions:

Preheat the griddle to HIGH.

Thread scallops, peppers, and onions on skewers.

Brush skewers with oil.

Grill for 10-12 minutes, flipping halfway, until scallops reach 130°F internal temperature.

Rest for 2 minutes before serving.

Nutrition Facts (1 portion):

Energy: 200 Kcal

Carbs: 22g

Proteins: 16g

Fats: 6g

Grilled Oysters

Portion Size: 2

Duration: 20 min

Ingredients:

6 Live Oysters

Instructions:

Preheat the griddle to HIGH.

Rinse oysters and place them on the griddle, flat side up.

Grill for 6-8 minutes until they open.

Remove from griddle and serve immediately.

Nutrition Facts (1 portion):

Energy: 25 Kcal

Carbs: 1g

Proteins: 3g

Fats: 1g

Grilled Lemon-Garlic Salmon

Portion Size: 2

Duration: 20 min

Ingredients:

2 Salmon fillets (6 oz. each)

1 tbsp Olive oil

2 Garlic cloves, minced

1/2 Lemon, juiced and zested

Salt and pepper, to taste

Fresh dill, for garnish

Instructions:

Preheat your Blackstone Griddle to medium-high heat.

In a small bowl, mix olive oil, garlic, lemon juice, zest, salt, and pepper.

Brush the salmon fillets with the lemon-garlic mixture on both sides.

Place salmon on the griddle, skin side down, and cook for about 4-5 minutes.

Gently flip the salmon and cook for another 4-5 minutes or until it's cooked to your desired doneness.

Garnish with fresh dill and serve with a lemon wedge.

Nutrition Facts (1 portion):

Energy: 367 Kcal

Carbs: 1g

Proteins: 34g

Fats: 24g

Sea Scallops Brochette with Pernod Sauce

Portion Size: 2

Duration: 20 min

Ingredients:

8 Sea Scallops

2 tbsp Pernod

4 tbsp Light Sour Cream

2 Fresh Rosemary Stalks

1/2 Tbsp Olive Oil

Salt and Pepper to taste

Instructions:

Clean scallops and pat dry.

Skewer scallops onto rosemary stalks.

Cook scallop skewers on the griddle with olive oil for 2 minutes each side.

Season with salt and pepper and set aside.

Deglaze the griddle with Pernod and add sour cream to create the sauce.

Serve scallops with the Pernod sauce.

Nutrition Facts (1 portion):

Energy: 64 Kcal

Carbs: 1.8g

Proteins: 1g

Fats: 6g

Blackstone Shrimp Tacos

Portion Size: 2 ***Duration:*** 15 min

Ingredients:

1/2 lb Shrimp, peeled and deveined

1 tsp Chili powder

1/2 tsp Cumin

1/2 tsp Garlic powder

Salt and pepper, to taste

4 Corn tortillas

1/2 cup Cabbage, shredded

1 Avocado, sliced

Lime wedges, for serving

Cilantro, for garnish

Instructions:

Preheat the Blackstone Griddle over medium heat.

Season shrimp with chili powder, cumin, garlic powder, salt, and pepper.

Place shrimp on the griddle and cook for 2-3 minutes per side until pink and cooked through.

Warm tortillas on the griddle for about 30 seconds per side.

Assemble tacos by placing shrimp on tortillas, topped with cabbage, avocado slices, and cilantro.

Serve with lime wedges on the side.

Nutrition Facts (1 portion):

Energy: 295 Kcal

Carbs: 20g

Proteins: 25g

Fats: 12g

Seafood Omelet

Portion Size: 2
Duration: 12 min

Ingredients:

1/2 Crab Meat

2 Green Onions

1 tsp Cheese

4 Eggs

Butter

Salt and Pepper to taste

Instructions:

Chop crab and onions.

Beat eggs.

Melt butter on the griddle.

Pour eggs, top with crab and onions.

Sprinkle cheese when almost done. Fold and serve.

Season with salt and pepper.

Nutrition Facts (1 portion):

Energy: 185 Kcal

Carbs: 11g

Proteins: 16g

Fats: 22g

Szechuan Shrimp with Mushrooms & Peppers

Portion Size: 2
Duration: 15 min

Ingredients:

1 Tbsp Soy Sauce

1 pkg Shiitake Mushrooms

1/4 cup Szechuan Sauce

1/2 Red Bell Pepper, diced

1 Tbsp Olive Oil

1 lb. Large Raw Shrimp

4 Green Onions, sliced

Salt and Pepper to taste

1/2 Tbsp Garlic Cheese Butter

Juice of 1/2 Lime

Instructions:

Mix Szechuan and soy sauce.

Heat oil on griddle. Cook mushrooms and pepper for 3 minutes.

Add shrimp, season with salt and pepper. Cook for 2 minutes.

Add onions, butter, and sauce. Cook until heated through.

Garnish with lime juice.

Nutrition Facts (1 portion):

Energy: 340 Kcal

Carbs: 13g

Proteins: 33g

Fats: 17g

Pan-Seared Salmon with Mustard Sauce

Portion Size: 2
Duration: 20 min

Ingredients:

2 (6 oz) Salmon Portions

Salt and Pepper to taste

1/2 Tbsp Olive Oil

1/4 cup Mustard Sauce

1/2 Tbsp Basting Oil

Pan Searing Flour (optional)

1/2 tsp Butter

Instructions:

Season salmon with salt and pepper.

Optional: Lightly coat with flour.

Heat olive oil on griddle. Cook salmon for 3 minutes per side.

Swirl in butter and basting oil.

Cook until salmon reaches 130°F. Rest for 2 minutes.

Serve with mustard sauce.

Nutrition Facts (1 portion):

Energy: 550 Kcal

Carbs: 1g

Proteins: 36g

Fats: 40g

Horseradish Crusted Salmon

Portion Size: 2
Duration: 25 min

Ingredients:

Olive Oil Spray

2 (6 oz) Salmon Portions

Salt and Pepper to taste

1/8 cup Basting Oil

1 Tbsp Prepared Horseradish

1/2 cup White Panko Bread Crumbs

2 tsp Horseradish Mustard

Instructions:

Preheat griddle to medium-high.

Season salmon with salt and pepper.

Combine panko, horseradish, and basting oil.

Spread mustard on salmon, top with breadcrumb mixture.

Bake for 14 minutes or until salmon reaches 130°F.

Rest for 2 minutes before serving.***Nutrition Facts (1 portion)***:

Energy: 490 Kcal

Carbs: 12g

Proteins: 37g

Fats: 30g

Salmon with Pesto

Portion Size: 2
Duration: 20 min

Ingredients:

2 (6 oz each) Fresh Skinless Atlantic Salmon Portions

4 Tbsp Basil Pesto Sauce, divided

4 Tbsp Shredded Parmigiano Reggiano, divided

2 Tbsp White Panko Bread Crumbs, divided

1/2 Tbsp Basting Oil

Instructions:

Preheat the Blackstone Griddle to medium-high.

Spread 2 Tbsp pesto evenly over each salmon portion.

Top each with 2 Tbsp shredded Parmigiano Reggiano and 1 Tbsp panko bread crumbs.

Drizzle basting oil on the griddle.

Place salmon, pesto side up, on the griddle.

Cook for about 8-10 minutes per side or until the internal temperature reaches 145°F and the crust is golden.

Nutrition Facts (1 portion):

Energy: 600 Kcal

Carbs: 5g

Proteins: 43g

Fats: 42g

Sea Bass with Citrus-Olive-Caper Sauce

Portion Size: 2
Duration: 20 min

Ingredients:

1 Skinned Sea Bass Fillet
1/8 tsp Black Pepper
1/3 cup Olive Oil
1/2 Tbsp Capers, rinsed
1/4 tsp Salt
1/2 Lemon, sliced
Lemon Juice
1 Tbsp Fresh Oregano, chopped
1/5 cup Chopped Olives

Instructions:

Preheat the Blackstone Griddle to high.

Brush the fillets with 1 tablespoon of oil on both sides and season with salt and pepper.

Place the fillets on the griddle, skin side down.

Cook for about 6 minutes, or until the skin is crisp and the fish is cooked through.

In a bowl, mix the lemon slices, juice, oregano, capers, olives, remaining oil, and seasonings.

Serve the sea bass topped with the citrus-olive-caper sauce.

Nutrition Facts (1 portion):

Energy: 231 Kcal

Carbs: 5g

Proteins: 26g

Fats: 11g

Burgers

Double Cheeseburger

Portion Size: 2

Duration: 25 min

Ingredients:

400 g Ground Beef

3 tsp Worcestershire Sauce

3 tsp Tomato Puree

2 tsp Mustard Powder

1 Crushed Garlic Clove

2 Cheddar Cheese Slices

2 Hamburger Buns, Halved

Salt & Black Pepper to Taste

Mayonnaise and Tomato Ketchup for Serving

Instructions:

Preheat Blackstone Griddle to medium-high.

Mix beef, Worcestershire sauce, tomato puree, mustard powder, garlic, salt, and pepper in a bowl. Shape into four patties.

Place patties on the griddle and cook for 2-3 minutes per side or until browned.

Add a cheese slice on top of each patty during the last minute of cooking.

Assemble burgers on buns with lettuce, tomato, mayonnaise, and ketchup.

Nutrition Facts (1 portion):

Energy: 655 Kcal

Carbs: 35g

Proteins: 40g

Fats: 45g

Mediterranean Turkey Burger

Portion Size: 2

Duration: 25 min

Ingredients:

2 Frozen Turkey Burgers

1 Roasted Red Pepper, Halved

2 English Muffins or Whole Grain Buns

Kalamata Olive Tapenade

1/4 Cup Cottage Cheese

1 Sun-Dried Tomato, Chopped

1/2 Garlic Clove, Chopped

1/8 Cup Chopped Cilantro

Salt & Pepper to Taste

Instructions:

Mix cottage cheese with tapenade ingredients in a blender to a thick paste.

Grill or fry turkey burgers on the griddle.

During the last minute of cooking, place a roasted red pepper half on each burger.

Toast buns on the griddle.

Spread tapenade on the bottom bun, top with burger and red pepper.

Add cheese sauce and cover with the top bun.

Nutrition Facts (1 portion):

Energy: 172 Kcal

Carbs: 30g

Proteins: 8.2g

Fats: 2.4g

Zinger Burger

Portion Size: 2

Duration: 50 min

Ingredients:

1 Chicken Breast

2 Hamburger Buns

Mayonnaise

Lettuce Leaves

Oil for Frying

Marinade: Salt, White Pepper, Black Pepper, 1 Egg, Red Chili Powder

Coating: Plain Flour, Corn Flour, Baking Powder, Salt & Black Pepper

Instructions:

Flatten chicken breast and marinate.

Coat chicken with flour mixture.

Fry chicken in oil on the griddle until golden and cooked through.

Toast buns with mayonnaise.

Assemble the burger with lettuce, chicken, and extra mayonnaisc.

Nutrition Facts (1 portion):

Energy: 380 Kcal

Carbs: 18g

Proteins: 27g

Fats: 6g

Spicy Mexican Bean Burger

Portion Size: 2
Duration: 15 min

Ingredients:

1/2 Can Vegan Refried Beans

1/2 Tsp Oil

1/4 Cup Minced Onion

1/4 Green Pepper, Diced

2 Burger Buns

1/2 Carrot, Shredded

Hot & Picante Sauce

1/2 Cup Breadcrumbs

1/4 Cup Flour

Salt, Black Pepper, Cumin, Pepper Flakes

1/4 Cup Sliced Black Olives

Instructions:

Sauté onion, green pepper, and carrot on the griddle.

Blend beans and cooked vegetables.

Add remaining **ingredients** and form into patties.

Cook patties on the griddle until browned on each side.

Serve with salsa, onion, and cheese on toasted buns.

Nutrition Facts (1 portion):

Energy: 313 Kcal

Carbs: 42g

Proteins: 7g

Fats: 12.9g

Bistro Burger

Portion Size: 2
Duration: 35 min

Ingredients:

2 Hamburger Buns

4 Slices Cheddar Cheese

1/2 Lb. Ground Sirloin

Salt & Black Pepper

Bistro Sauce: Mayonnaise, Dijon Mustard

Caramelized Onions: Sweet Onion, Brown Sugar

Ruffles Potato Chips

Instructions:

Preheat griddle.

Cook caramelized onions with butter, oil, and brown sugar.

Season and grill burgers until desired doneness.

Add cheese and onions in the last minute.

Assemble with bistro sauce and potato chips on buns.

Nutrition Facts (1 portion):
Energy: 689 Kcal
Carbs: 45g
Proteins: 43g
Fats: 36g

Cherry and Brie Burger

Portion Size: 2
Duration: 60 min

Ingredients:
400g Bison or Lean Ground Beef
1/4 Cup Bulgur Wheat or Fine Grain
1 Onion, Sliced
2 Garlic Cloves, Minced
2 Cups Dried Tart Cherries
8 oz Brie Cheese, Sliced
8 Hamburger Buns
Lettuce Leaves
4 Tbsp Olive Oil
Salt & Pepper to Taste

Instructions:
Preheat Blackstone Griddle.

Soak bulgur wheat in boiling water until absorbed, then microwave for 2-3 minutes.

Sauté onion in olive oil until golden, then cool.

In a bowl, mix mayonnaise, pepper, rosemary. Refrigerate.

In a food processor, blend cherries into a fine mixture.

Combine cherries, onion, bulgur, meat, salt, and pepper. Form into patties.

Grill patties, flipping once, until cooked through. Top with brie.

Grill buns and assemble burgers with mayo, lettuce, and grilled onions.

Nutrition Facts (1 portion):
Energy: 1900 Kcal
Carbs: 41g
Proteins: 124g
Fats: 137g

Veggie Tuna Burger

Portion Size: 2
Duration: 30 min

Ingredients:
1/2 Can Light Water-packed Tuna, Drained
1/2 Carrot, Shredded
1/2 Zucchini, Shredded
1/2 Summer Squash, Shredded
1/3 Egg, Beaten
2/3 Cups Soft Whole Wheat Bread Crumbs
Salt & Pepper to Taste
2 Hamburger Buns
2 Slices Low-fat Cheddar Cheese
Lettuce & Tomato Slices

Instructions:
Sauté onion and garlic, then add carrots, zucchini, and squash until tender.

In a bowl, mix egg, bread crumbs, tuna, sautéed vegetables, salt, and pepper.

Form into patties and cook in butter until browned.

Serve on buns with cheese, lettuce, and tomato.

Nutrition Facts (1 portion):
Energy: 433 Kcal
Carbs: 74g
Proteins: 18g
Fats: 6g

Chicken Burger

Portion Size: 2
Duration: 40 min

Ingredients:
400g Minced Chicken
4 Tbsp Ketchup
4 Tbsp Mustard
1 Garlic Clove, Minced
1/3 Onion, Minced
Salt & Pepper to Taste

Instructions:
Sauté onion and garlic until softened.
Combine chicken, ketchup, mustard, salt, pepper, sautéed onion, and garlic.
Form into patties and cook on a greased griddle until done.

Nutrition Facts (1 portion):
Energy: 334 Kcal
Carbs: 14g
Proteins: 27g
Fats: 19g

Smash Burger

Portion Size: 2

Duration: 25 min

Ingredients:
250g Steak Mince
2 Burger Buns
2 Slices Cheddar Cheese
1 Red Onion, Finely Chopped
1 Tomato, Sliced
Mayonnaise, Ketchup
Shredded Iceberg Lettuce

Instructions:
Toast buns and set aside.
Season mince and form into two heaps. Place on a hot griddle and smash into thin patties.
Cook for 2 minutes each side, topping with cheese.
Assemble burgers with lettuce, onion, tomato, and sauces.

Nutrition Facts (1 portion):
Energy: 666 Kcal
Carbs: 41g
Proteins: 37g
Fats: 39g

Chicken Caesar Burger

Portion Size: 2
Duration: 30 min

Ingredients:
1/2 Lb Chicken Mince
2 Tbsp Parmesan Cheese, Divided
1 Tbsp Lemon Juice
1 1/2 Tbsp Parsley Flakes
1 Garlic Clove, Minced
1 Tbsp Worcestershire Sauce
Salt & Pepper to Taste

2 Hamburger Buns

Shredded Romaine Lettuce

4 Tbsp Caesar Salad Dressing

Instructions:

Mix onion, cheese, parsley, garlic, lemon juice, Worcestershire, salt, and pepper.

Add chicken and form into patties.

Cook patties until internal temp reaches 165°F.

Assemble on buns with dressing and romaine.

Nutrition Facts (1 portion):

Energy: 467 Kcal

Carbs: 40g

Proteins: 30g

Fats: 20g

Spinach Feta Burger

Portion Size: 2

Duration: 20 min

Ingredients:

1 Cup Fresh Spinach, Torn

1/8 Cup Feta Cheese Crumbles

1/8 Cup Plum Tomatoes, Finely Sliced

1/2 Green Onion, Chopped

1/4 Tsp Dill

1/4 Tsp Pepper & Salt

1/2 Lbs Ground Beef

2 Hamburger Buns

Instructions:

Mix spinach, feta, tomatoes, green onion, dill, pepper, salt, and ground beef in a bowl.

Form into two 4-inch patties.

Grill on the Blackstone Griddle over medium heat for 4-5 minutes each side until internal temp reaches 160°F.

Serve on split hamburger buns.

Nutrition Facts (1 portion):

Energy: 446 Kcal

Carbs: 37g

Proteins: 30g

Fats: 20g

Chicken Cheese Burger

Portion Size: 2

Duration: 20 min

Ingredients:

2 Burger Buns

2 Slices Cheddar Cheese

1/8 Cup Ranch Dressing

1 Chicken Breast, Halved

1/8 Cup Salsa Sauce

2 Lettuce Leaves

Instructions:

Cook chicken on a preheated Blackstone Griddle until fully cooked.

Toast burger buns lightly.

Spread ranch dressing on the bottom bun.

Layer with lettuce, cooked chicken, salsa, and cheese.

Top with the other half of the bun and serve.

Nutrition Facts (1 portion):

Energy: 446 Kcal

Carbs: 32g

Proteins: 27g

Fats: 14g

Tandoori Chicken Burger

Portion Size: 2
Duration: 45 min

Ingredients:

2 Chicken Breast Fillets
1 Tbsp Tandoori Masala Powder
1/4 Cup Plain Yogurt
3 Tsps Mint Leaves, Chopped
2 Burger Buns
1 Tomato, Thinly Sliced
1 Onion, Diced
1 Carrot, Finely Cut
1 Cup Mixed Salad Leaves
1/2 Tbsp Oil

Instructions:

Mix tandoori masala with water and yogurt. Marinate chicken in this mixture for 5-10 minutes.

Grill chicken on Blackstone Griddle until cooked.

Toast buns if desired. Spread yogurt and mint mixture on buns.

Assemble with lettuce, salad leaves, cucumber, carrots, onions, and cooked chicken patty.

Serve immediately.

Nutrition Facts (1 portion):

Energy: 465 Kcal
Carbs: 35g
Proteins: 25g
Fats: 28g

Chicken Cordon Bleu Burger

Portion Size: 2

Duration: 30 min

Ingredients:

2 Tbsp Sour Cream
1 Tbsp Yellow Mustard
1/10 Cup Honey
1 Boneless Chicken Breast Half, Flattened
2 Slices Swiss Cheese
2 Slices Deli Ham
2 Onion Buns

Instructions:

Preheat Blackstone Griddle. Mix honey, mustard, and sour cream; refrigerate.

Season chicken with onion powder. Cook in a until browned. Top with cheese and ham.

Toast buns on the griddle. Assemble burgers with honey-mustard sauce.

Nutrition Facts (1 portion):

Energy: 673 Kcal
Carbs: 50g
Proteins: 66g
Fats: 25g

Turkey Burger with Special Sauce

Portion Size: 2
Duration: 25 min

Ingredients:

1/8 Cup Green Onions, Minced
1 Tbsp Orange Juice
1/2 Tbsp Soy Sauce
1/2 Tsp Ginger, Peeled and Chopped
1/2 Garlic Clove, Minced
1/2 Lb Ground Turkey Breast
1/8 Cup Special Sauce
2 Whole Wheat Hamburger Buns

2 Lettuce Leaves

Instructions:

Preheat Blackstone Griddle.

Mix green onions, orange juice, soy sauce, ginger, garlic, and ground turkey.

Form into patties and cook on the griddle until done.

Serve on buns with special sauce and lettuce.

Nutrition Facts (1 portion):

Energy: 301 Kcal

Carbs: 18g

Proteins: 27g

Fats: 7g

Vegan Black Bean Burger

Portion Size: 2
Duration: 65 min

Ingredients:

1/4 Tsp Egg Substitute

1/4 Tbsp Water

1/8 Tsp Each Cumin, Onion, and Garlic Powder

1/10 Can Refried Beans

1/10 Tsp Chipotle Powder

1 1/2 Cup Chopped Mushrooms

1/8 Whole Onion, Diced and Sautéed

1/5 Cup Whole Wheat Breadcrumbs

1/8 Can Black Beans, Rinsed

Instructions:

Preheat oven to 350°F.

Blend ingredients. Form into patties and place on a baking sheet.

Bake for 15 minutes, flip, then bake for another 10 minutes.

Serve with your favorite toppings and buns.

Nutrition Facts (1 portion):

Energy: 80 Kcal

Carbs: 13g

Proteins: 5g

Fats: 1.3g

Steakhouse Burger

Portion Size: 2
Duration: 25 min

Ingredients:

2 Pieces Sandwich Bread

1/3 Cup Milk

1/2 Tsp Each Kosher Salt and Black Pepper

1 Garlic Clove, Minced

1/2 Tbsp Worcestershire Sauce

1 Tsp Ketchup

1 Lb Lean Beef

2 Hamburger Buns

Instructions:

Preheat Blackstone Griddle.

Mix bread and milk, then add Worcestershire, ketchup, salt, pepper, and garlic. Mix well.

Add beef and form into patties.

Grill patties until desired doneness. Toast buns on the griddle.

Serve burgers on buns.

Nutrition Facts (1 portion):

Energy: 517 Kcal

Carbs: 28g

Proteins: 38g

Fats: 27g

Burger with Grilled Onion

Portion Size: 2
Duration: 30 min

Ingredients:
1/2 lb. Minced Beef
2 Hamburger Buns, Split & Toasted
1 Large Sweet Onion, Sliced
Lettuce Leaves
Tomato Slices
Oil
Salt & Pepper to Taste

Instructions:
Form minced beef into two 3/4-inch thick patties.

Brush onion slices with oil.

Grill patties and onion slices on the Blackstone Griddle over medium heat until burgers reach 160°F, flipping once.

Season burgers and onions with salt and pepper.

Assemble burgers with lettuce, tomatoes, and grilled onions on toasted buns.

Nutrition Facts (1 portion):
Energy: 553 Kcal
Carbs: 43g
Proteins: 40g
Fats: 25g

Homemade Beef Burger

Portion Size: 2
Duration: 35 min

Ingredients:
1 Small Egg, Beaten
1/2 Onion, Chopped
1 Tsp Olive Oil
250g Beef Steak Mince
1/2 Tsp Mixed Dried Herbs
2 White Rolls
Lettuce Leaves
1/2 Beef Tomato, Sliced

Instructions:
Sauté onion in olive oil until softened and browned.

Mix egg, herbs, and beef mince together. Season and add onions.

Form into two patties.

Grill on the Blackstone Griddle until cooked.

Serve on toasted buns with lettuce and tomato slices.

Nutrition Facts (1 portion):
Energy: 472 Kcal
Carbs: 29g
Proteins: 32g
Fats: 26g

Zesty Onion Burger

Portion Size: 2
Duration: 35 min

Ingredients:
1/2 lb. Beef Mince
1 Cup Celery, Sliced
1/2 Can Condensed Onion Soup
1/8 Cup Water
1/8 Cup Ketchup
1/2 Tsp Worcestershire Sauce
1/8 Tsp Mustard
1/8 Tsp Pepper

3 Hamburger Buns, Split
1 Tbsp Butter, Softened

Instructions:

Sauté beef and celery. Drain.

Add ketchup, mustard, Worcestershire, pepper, soup, and water.

Bring to a boil, then simmer until thickened.

Toast buns with butter. Add meat mixture on top.

Nutrition Facts (1 portion):

Energy: 683 Kcal

Carbs: 64g

Proteins: 34g

Fats: 33g

Chicken Chili Burger

Portion Size: 2
Duration: 45 min

Ingredients:

1 1/2 lb. Chicken Cutlets

1/4 Bell Pepper, Finely Chopped

3 Tbsp Chili Sauce

Oil for Griddle

8 oz Cheddar Cheese, Sliced

2 Hamburger Buns

1/4 Large Red Onion, Sliced

2 Lettuce Leaves

Instructions:

Process chicken cutlets in a food processor, then mix with bell pepper, cilantro, and chili sauce.

Form into two patties.

Grill on Blackstone Griddle until cooked.

Top with cheese in the last few minutes.

Serve on buns with lettuce and onion.

Nutrition Facts (1 portion):

Energy: 576 Kcal

Carbs: 64g

Proteins: 25g

Fats: 22g

Chicken Parmesan Burger

Portion Size: 2
Duration: 35 min

Ingredients:

2 Burger Buns

1/4 Cup Parmesan Cheese, Grated

2 Tbsp Basil, Chopped

3/4 Cup Marinara Sauce

6 oz Ground White Chicken

1 Tbsp Olive Oil

1/2 Tbsp Onion, Grated

2 oz Mozzarella Cheese, Sliced

Salt to Taste

2 Large Radish Leaves

Instructions:

Process Parmesan and basil in a food processor.

Mix marinara and basil in a pot, adding some to the ground chicken.

Form into two patties and grill on the Blackstone Griddle.

Serve on buns with radish leaves and marinara sauce.

Nutrition Facts (1 portion):

Energy: 554 Kcal

Carbs: 38g

Proteins: 35g

Fats: 28g

Zeus Burger

Portion Size: 2

Duration: 35 min

Ingredients:

1 1/2 Tbsp Fat-Free Mayonnaise

1/2 Tsp Garlic, Minced

1/8 Tsp Dried Oregano

1/2 lb Lean Ground Beef

2 Hamburger Buns, Split

2 Tbsp Spinach, Chopped & Thawed

2 Tbsp Feta Cheese, Crumbled

1 Tsp Lemon Juice

1 Tsp Pine Nuts, Chopped

1/2 Tsp Garlic & Dried Oregano

1/8 Tsp Salt

1/2 Tsp Pepper

Instructions:

Mix mayonnaise, garlic, oregano, lemon juice, and salt.

Combine spinach, cheese, lemon juice, pine nuts, oregano, salt, pepper, and beef.

Form into patties and grill on the Blackstone Griddle.

Serve on buns with prepared sauce.

Nutrition Facts (1 portion):

Energy: 425 Kcal

Carbs: 40g

Proteins: 33g

Fats: 14g

Greek Style Chicken Burger

Portion Size: 2

Duration: 35 min

Ingredients:

1/2 lb Ground Chicken

1/6 Cup Breadcrumbs

1/2 Egg

1 Tbsp Milk

1/2 Tbsp Lime Juice

1/8 Tsp Salt & Pepper

1 Tbsp Vegetable Oil

2 Burger Buns

Mayonnaise for Burgers

2 Red Onion Slices

2 Tomato Slices

2 Lettuce Leaves

Instructions:

Mix chicken, breadcrumbs, egg, milk, lime juice, salt, and pepper.

Form into patties and cook on Blackstone Griddle.

Serve on buns with mayonnaise, lettuce, tomato, and onion.

Nutrition Facts (1 portion):

Energy: 382 Kcal

Carbs: 32g

Proteins: 28g

Fats: 14g

Cheddar Chicken Burger

Portion Size: 2

Duration: 20 min

Ingredients:

1/2 lb Ground Chicken

1 Clove Garlic, Minced

1/2 Tbsp Worcestershire Sauce

1/4 Cup Cheddar Cheese, Diced

1/2 Tbsp Canola Oil

2 Hamburger Buns

Toppings of Choice

Instructions:

Mix ground chicken with garlic, Worcestershire sauce, and cheddar cheese.

Form into patties and cook in canola oil on Blackstone Griddle.

Serve on buns with preferred toppings.

Nutrition Facts (1 portion):

Energy: 270 Kcal

Carbs: 3g

Proteins: 25g

Fats: 18g

Pork

Pork Chops

Portion Size: 2
Duration: 40 min

Ingredients:

1 Pork Chop
Chicken Seasoning, a pinch
2 Tbsp Melted Butter
2 oz Cream of Mushroom Soup
1 Tbsp Chopped Frozen Onions
2 Tbsp Milk
2 Tbsp Water

Instructions:

Preheat the Blackstone Griddle to medium heat.

Brush the pork chop with melted butter and sprinkle with chicken seasoning.

Place the pork chop on the griddle and cook for 20 minutes on each side.

In a bowl, mix cream of mushroom soup, onions, milk, and water. Pour this mixture over the pork chop during the last 10 minutes of cooking.

Serve hot.

Nutrition Facts (1 portion):

Energy: 60 Kcal
Carbs: 1.3g
Proteins: 0.11g
Fats: 5.9g

Pork Loin Crunch in Red Wine

Portion Size: 2
Duration: 40 min

Ingredients:

1 lb. Pork Loin Roast
Basil, a pinch
Pepper Powder, a pinch
Fresh Garlic, minced, a pinch
Nutmeg, a pinch
2 Tbsp Red Wine
1 Tbsp Olive Oil
Water as needed
2 Tbsp Bran Flakes (Cereal)

Instructions:

Mix garlic, basil, pepper, and nutmeg. Rub onto the pork loin.

Crush bran flakes and coat the pork loin.

Preheat the Blackstone Griddle to medium and drizzle with olive oil.

Place the pork loin on the griddle, add red wine and a little water around it.

Cook for 35-40 minutes, turning occasionally.

Let it rest before slicing. Serve with the pan juices.

Nutrition Facts (1 portion):

Energy: 398 Kcal
Carbs: 5.47g
Proteins: 54g
Fats: 15.5g

Pork Taquitos

Portion Size: 2
Duration: 50 min

Ingredients:

1/6 Medium Onion, Minced
Canola Oil, a splash
1/3 Garlic Clove, Minced

1/3 tsp Cumin Powder

Ground Chili, a dash

Cayenne Pepper, a dash

1/3 cup Cooked and Shredded Pork

Shredded Mexican Cheese, a handful

Fresh Cilantro, a sprinkle

Verde Salsa, a dollop

2 Corn Tortillas, warmed

Instructions:

Preheat the Blackstone Griddle to medium heat.

Sauté onion and garlic with a splash of canola oil.

Add cumin, chili powder, and cayenne pepper.

Mix in the pork, cheese, cilantro, and salsa. Cook until the cheese melts.

Spread the filling on tortillas and roll tightly. Secure with toothpicks.

Grill the taquitos on the griddle until crispy.

Serve hot with sour cream.

Nutrition Facts (1 portion):

Energy: 197 Kcal

Carbs: 13g

Proteins: 12g

Fats: 11g

Pork Tenderloin Stir Fry with Tangerines

Portion Size: 2

Duration: 25 min

Ingredients:

5/8 lb. Pork Tenderloin, sliced

1/2 Tbsp Corn Flour

1 Tbsp Asian Sesame Oil

1/2 Tbsp Fresh Ginger, chopped

2 Clementines, diced

2 Tbsps. Chili Sauce

1 Tbsp Soy Sauce

Chinese Five-Spice Powder, a pinch

3 Baby Bok Choy, diced

2 ½ Onions, thinly sliced

Instructions:

Coat pork slices with corn flour.

Heat sesame oil on the griddle. Add ginger and pork. Cook until browned.

Add tangerines, chili sauce, soy sauce, and five-spice powder. Stir well.

Add bok choy and onions, stir-frying until wilted.

Serve hot.

Nutrition Facts (1 portion):

Energy: 253 Kcal

Carbs: 7.6g

Proteins: 37g

Fats: 9.6g

Pulled Pork Sandwich

Portion Size: 2

Duration: 30 min

Ingredients:

6 oz Cooked and Shredded Pork

1/2 cup Low Sodium Chicken Broth

1 Tbsp Balsamic Vinegar

1 Tbsp Brown Sugar

1/2 tsp Chili Powder

1/2 tsp Paprika

1/2 tsp Cumin

Dash of Salt

1/8 tsp Black Pepper

2 Kaiser Rolls, Split

Instructions:

Combine pork, broth, spices, vinegar, and sugar on the griddle.

Simmer until the sauce thickens.

Serve on split Kaiser rolls.

Nutrition Facts (1 portion):

Energy: 458 Kcal

Carbs: 37g

Proteins: 28g

Fats: 20g

Pork Sausage Gravy

Portion Size: 2

Duration: 30 min

Ingredients:

1/2 lb. Ground Pork Sausage

1/2 cups Milk

Flour as needed

Salt and Pepper to Taste

Instructions:

Brown sausage on the griddle. Set aside.

Add flour to drippings to make a roux. Gradually add milk to form a creamy gravy.

Return sausage to the griddle, seasoning with salt and pepper.

Nutrition Facts (1 portion):

Energy: 408 Kcal

Carbs: 11g

Proteins: 20g

Fats: 30g

Pork Sausage with Lentils

Portion Size: 2

Duration: 45 min

Ingredients:

Olive Oil, as needed

2 oz. Pancetta, diced

1 Yellow Onion, chopped

6 Pork Sausages

4 oz Mushrooms, chopped

2 Garlic Cloves, minced

3/4 cups Brown Lentils

Basil, chopped, as needed

1/4 cup White Wine

1 cup Chicken Broth

1 cup Baby Spinach Leaves

Salt and Pepper to Taste

Instructions:

Heat oil on the griddle. Cook pancetta until crispy. Set aside.

Sauté onions, then add sausages. Cook until browned.

Add garlic, mushrooms, basil, lentils, wine, and broth.

Cover and simmer. Add spinach at the end.

Serve with fresh bread.

Nutrition Facts (1 portion):

Energy: 1440 Kcal

Carbs: 56g

Proteins: 85g

Fats: 85g

Pork Chops and Apple Bake

Portion Size: 2

Duration: 70 min

Ingredients:

2 Pork Chops

Wheat Germ, as needed

2/5 Egg

Seasonings: Garlic Powder, Basil, Rosemary

Balsamic Vinegar, as needed

Cinnamon, a pinch

1 Apple, sliced

Water as needed

Salt and Pepper

Instructions:

Mix eggs in a bowl. Combine wheat germ and seasonings in another bowl.

Coat pork chops with egg, then wheat germ mixture.

Cook on the Blackstone Griddle with a splash of water and balsamic vinegar.

Add apple slices during the last 15 minutes. Serve with your choice of sides.

Nutrition Facts (1 portion):

Energy: 168 Kcal

Carbs: 30g

Proteins: 6.6g

Fats: 3.7g

Pork Stew

Portion size: 2

Preparation: 10 minutes

Duration: 20-25 minutes

Ingredients:

1 lb boneless pork shoulder, thinly sliced

1/2 medium sweet onion, diced

1 large carrot, grated

1/2 cup chopped celery

1/8 cup tomato paste

1 clove garlic, minced

1/2 Tbsp Better Than Bouillon® mushroom base

1 cup water

1/2 Tbsp olive oil

1/4 sprig fresh rosemary (optional)

Salt and pepper to taste

Instructions:

Preheat your Blackstone griddle to medium-high heat.

Drizzle olive oil on the griddle and sear the pork in batches until golden brown. Transfer cooked pork to a plate.

Add onions to the griddle and cook until softened, about 5 minutes. Stir in garlic, carrots, and celery until heated through.

Mix in tomato paste and mushroom base, coating the vegetables.

Pour in water and add the cooked pork (with any juices) back to the griddle. Nestled the rosemary sprig (if using).

Bring to a simmer, then reduce heat to low and cook for 15-20 minutes, stirring occasionally, until thickened and flavors meld.

Season with salt and pepper to taste.

Nutritional Info (per serving, estimated):

Calories: 320

Carbs: 15g

Protein: 40g

Fat: 10g

Pork Chow Mein

Portion size: 2 hungry bellies

Preparation: 5 minutes

Duration: 15 minutes

Ingredients:

2 Tbsp vegetable oil

1/2 cup sliced onions & celery

1 cup cooked pork, diced (leftovers, grilled, or boiled)

1 Tbsp soy sauce

1 cup bean sprouts, drained (optional)

1 Tbsp cornstarch mixed with 2 Tbsp water

2 cups chicken or vegetable broth

Cooked rice or noodles

Instructions:

Crank your Blackstone griddle to medium-high heat.

Drizzle oil and toss in onions and celery. Stir-fry for 3-4 minutes, until slightly softened.

Add the cooked pork and soy sauce. Cook for 1 minute, scraping up any browned bits.

Toss in the bean sprouts (if using).

Pour in the broth and cornstarch mixture, stirring constantly until thickened.

Cook for another minute until heated through.

Serve it up:

Pile onto your favorite cooked rice or noodles.

Garnish with chopped green onions or sesame seeds for an extra kick.

Nutritional Info (per serving, estimated):

Calories: 330

Carbs: 20g

Protein: 25g

Fat: 15g

Sizzling Pork Chops with Veggies

Portion size: 2

Preparation: 5 minutes

Duration: 20 minutes

Ingredients:

1/2 teaspoon canola oil

2 bone-in pork chops, center-cut, 6 ounces each

1/2 teaspoon salt

1 cup carrots, sliced diagonally

1/2 cup frozen pearl onions, thawed

1 teaspoon all-purpose flour

1/2 cup unsalted chicken broth

1 teaspoon Dijon mustard

1/2 teaspoon black pepper

1 tablespoon unsalted butter, chopped

Instructions:

Preheat your Blackstone griddle to medium-high heat.

Drizzle oil on the griddle and heat it up.

Sprinkle pork chops with half the salt (1/4 teaspoon each). Sear for 3 minutes per side until nicely browned. Transfer cooked chops to a plate.

Add carrots and onions to the griddle and cook for 3 minutes, stirring occasionally.

Sprinkle flour over the vegetables and cook for 30 seconds, stirring constantly.

In a separate bowl, whisk together chicken broth, Dijon mustard, and remaining salt (1/4 teaspoon).

Pour the broth mixture onto the griddle and bring to a simmer. Scrape up any browned bits from the bottom.

Return the pork chops to the griddle and cover with the sauce. Add black pepper.

Simmer for 2-3 minutes, or until sauce thickens slightly, pork is heated through, and carrots are tender.

Remove from heat and drizzle with chopped butter.

Nutritional Info (per serving, estimated):
Calories: 300
Carbs: 15g
Protein: 35g
Fat: 10g

Garlic Lime Pork with Spinach

Portion size: 2 happy bellies
Preparation: 5 minutes
Duration: 25 minutes

Ingredients:
1 tablespoon lime juice
1/2 tablespoon almond or peanut butter
2 cloves garlic, minced
Salt and pepper to taste
1 teaspoon honey
2 bone-in pork chops (8 ounces each), trimmed and chopped
2 teaspoons olive oil
1 bag (2 ounces) fresh baby spinach
Optional: Lime wedges, chopped walnuts

Instructions:
In a small bowl, whisk together lime juice, peanut butter, garlic, salt, pepper, and honey.

Sprinkle pork chops with 1/8 teaspoon each of salt and pepper.

Heat 2 tablespoons olive oil on the Blackstone griddle over medium-high heat.

Add the pork chops and cook for 7-10 minutes, flipping once. Transfer cooked chops to a plate and cover to keep warm.

Reduce heat to medium-low and add the remaining 2 tablespoons olive oil to the griddle.

Whisk any browned bits from the bottom of the griddle into the oil.

Add the spinach and sauté until wilted and cooked through, about 2-3 minutes. Season with additional pepper if desired.

Plate the pork chops and top with the spinach. Serve with lime wedges and chopped walnuts if using.

Nutritional Info (per serving, estimated):
Calories: 350
Carbs: 20g
Protein: 40g
Fat: 10g

Pork Chops with Garlicky Broccoli

Portion Size: 2
Duration: 30 min

Ingredients:
1 lb. Spear-Shaped Broccoli
3 Tbsp Olive Oil
1/2 cup Panko Breadcrumbs
1 Tbsp Parmesan Cheese
1 Tbsp Whole Wheat Flour
1 Small Egg, Slightly Beaten
2 Boneless Pork Chops (2 oz each)
1/4 tsp Salt & Red Pepper
2 Garlic Cloves, Sliced
1 Tbsp Red Wine Vinegar

Instructions:
Preheat Blackstone Griddle to high.
Cook broccoli with 1 Tbsp oil until slightly blackened.

In a shallow dish, mix breadcrumbs and Parmesan.

In another dish, mix egg and flour.

Season pork with salt and coat in flour, then breadcrumbs.

Cook pork chops in 1 Tbsp oil until golden brown and 145°F internal temp.

Set pork aside and cover with foil.

In the same griddle, cook garlic and red pepper in 1 tsp oil.

Remove from heat, add vinegar and remaining salt.

Toss broccoli in garlic mixture and serve with pork chops.

Nutrition Facts (1 portion):
Energy: 543 Kcal

Carbs: 21g

Proteins: 34g

Fats: 37g

Pork Pot Pie

Portion Size: 2

Duration: 40 min

Ingredients:
1 Medium Carrot, Thinly Sliced

1/2 Onion, Chopped

1/8 Cup Water

1 Cup Cooked Pork Cubes

1/2 Can Cream of Celery Soup

1 Tbsp Fresh Parsley

1/8 tsp Salt & Garlic Powder

Pie Crust for 9-Inch Pie

Parmesan Cheese

Instructions:

Cook carrots and onion in water on griddle until soft.

Add soup, pork, parsley, salt, and garlic powder.

Transfer to a 9-inch pie dish.

Roll out pastry and cover the mixture.

Make slits in the top and add Parmesan.

Cook on griddle with a cover or foil until golden brown.

Let stand for 5 minutes before serving.

Nutrition Facts (1 portion):
Energy: 609 Kcal

Carbs: 25g

Proteins: 34g

Fats: 40g

Pork Rice Stir-Fry

Portion Size: 2

Duration: 20 min

Ingredients:
2 oz. Pork Tenderloin, Diced

2 tsp Canola Oil

1/4 Cup Fresh Mushrooms

1/4 Cup Sugar Snap Peas

1 Tbsp Red & Green Pepper

1/2 Tbsp Green Onion

1/8 tsp Minced Garlic

1/2 Tbsp Soy Sauce

1/8 tsp Sugar

1/2 Cup Leftover Rice

Instructions:
Fry pork in oil on the griddle until brown.

Remove pork and add remaining oil.

Add vegetables, garlic, soy sauce, and sugar.

Cook until veggies are crisp-tender.
Return pork to griddle and add rice.
Cook until heated through.

Nutrition Facts (1 portion):
Energy: 184 Kcal
Carbs: 22g
Proteins: 9.6g
Fats: 6.3g

BBQ Pork Chops

Portion Size: 2
Duration: 100 min

Ingredients:
1/3 Pork Chop
1/3 Spanish Onion
1 Tbsp Brown Sugar
1/8 Cup Ketchup
1/4 Cup Water

Instructions:
Grill pork chops on the griddle, topping with onion slice and brown sugar.
Mix ketchup and water.
Pour over pork chops and cover.
Cook for 90 minutes at medium heat on the griddle.
Serve hot.

Nutrition Facts (1 portion):
Energy: 88 Kcal
Carbs: 11g
Proteins: 0.78g
Fats: 4.16g

Shredded Pork Tacos

Portion Size: 2
Duration: 170 min

Ingredients:
1/2 lb Pork Loin
1 Garlic Clove, Minced
1 tsp Cumin
1/4 Cup Onion
1/2 Tbsp Apple Cider Vinegar
1 Tbsp Olive Oil
1 Tbsp Chipotle Chilies Puree
1/8 Cup Cilantro
1 Tbsp Water

Instructions:
Mix all ingredients on the griddle and cook until pork is tender.
Shred pork and serve on tortillas with toppings.

Nutrition Facts (1 portion):
Energy: 312 Kcal
Carbs: 3.4g
Proteins: 24g
Fats: 10g

Chinese Pork Tenderloin

Portion Size: 2
Duration: 45 min

Ingredients:
2/3 Pork Tenderloins
2 tsp Light Soy Sauce
1/3 cup Sherry
1 tsp Black Bean Sauce
1/2 tsp Fresh Ginger, Minced

1/2 tsp Brown Sugar

1/3 Garlic Clove, Minced

1/6 tsp Sesame Oil

1/3 Pinch Chinese Five-Spice Powder

Instructions:

Marinate tenderloins with soy sauce, sherry, black bean sauce, ginger, sugar, garlic, sesame oil, and five-spice powder for 2-24 hours.

Preheat Blackstone griddle to medium-high.

Grill tenderloins for 30-35 minutes or until desired doneness.

Let rest for 10 minutes, then slice diagonally.

Nutrition Facts (1 portion):

Energy: 195 Kcal

Carbs: 4.6g

Proteins: 35g

Fats: 3.5g

BBQ Pulled Tuna Sandwich

Portion Size: 2

Duration: 20 min

Ingredients:

1/4 cup Red Onion Slices

1 Garlic Clove, Minced

1/2 tbsp Water

1 1/2 (6 oz.) cans Pork, Drained

1/2 tsp Worcestershire Sauce

1/2 tbsp Steak Spice

1/2 cup BBQ Sauce

1/8 cup Butter

2 Large Soft Rolls, Warmed

Instructions:

Cook onion and garlic with water on griddle until soft.

Add Worcestershire sauce, tuna, and steak seasoning.

Stir in BBQ sauce and simmer for 5 minutes.

Butter the rolls and top with the tuna mixture.

Nutrition Facts (1 portion):

Energy: 252 Kcal

Carbs: 25g

Proteins: 13g

Fats: 11g

Pork Sandwich Spread

Portion Size: 2

Duration: 15 min

Ingredients:

2/3 cup Cooked Ground Pork

2 Tbsp Minced Celery & Mayo

1/3 tbsp Sweet Pickle & Chopped Onion

Pepper, to Taste

1/3 tbsp Mustard

4 Slices White Bread

Instructions:

Mix pork, celery, mayo, pickle, onion, pepper, and mustard.

Spread mixture on bread slices to make sandwiches.

Nutrition Facts (1 portion):

Energy: 503 Kcal

Carbs: 27g

Proteins: 27g

Fats: 31g

Pork Sausage Patties

Portion Size: 2
Duration: 30 min

Ingredients:
1/3 Beaten Egg
1/8 cup Milk
2 Tbsp Minced Onion
2/3 Tbsp All-Purpose Flour
Salt & Pepper, as desired
1 lb Bulk Sage Pork Sausage

Instructions:
Mix egg, milk, onion, flour, salt, and pepper.
Add sausage and form into six patties.
Cook on preheated griddle for 6 minutes each side.

Nutrition Facts (1 portion):
Energy: 32.6 Kcal
Carbs: 4.1g
Proteins: 1.7g
Fats: 0.33g

Pork Sausage and Apple Patties

Portion Size: 2
Duration: 30 min

Ingredients:
1/4 Apple, Sliced
1/2 cup Breadcrumbs
1/4 cup Celery, Sliced
1 tbsp Brown Sugar
1/2 lb Bulk Pork Sausage

Instructions:
Mix all ingredients and form into patties.

Cook on griddle at 350°F for 30 minutes.
Serve each patty on an apple ring.

Nutrition Facts (1 portion):
Energy: 433 Kcal
Carbs: 19g
Proteins: 27g
Fats: 26g

Pork Chops and Bean Bake

Portion Size: 2
Duration: 60 min

Ingredients:
2/3 can Tomato Beans
1 2/3 Lean Pork Chops
2 Tbsp Brown Sugar
2 Tbsp Ketchup
5-6 Onion Slices
5-6 Lemon Slices
Salt & Fresh Milled Black Pepper

Instructions:
Place beans in a griddle-safe baking dish.
Add chops on top, season with salt and pepper.
Apply mustard and brown sugar.
Top with ketchup and bake at 325°F for 1.25 hours without a lid.
Add onion and lemon slices, bake for 15 more minutes.

Nutrition Facts (1 portion):
Energy: 252 Kcal
Carbs: 56g
Proteins: 8.24g
Fats: 1.51g

Pork Lo Mein

Portion Size: 2
Duration: 20 min

Ingredients:

1/2 lb. Pork Tenderloin
1/8 cup Low Sodium Soy Sauce
1 1/2 Minced Garlic Cloves
1 tsp Fresh Ginger, Chopped
1/8 tsp Red Pepper Flakes
1 cup Fresh Snow Peas
1/2 Medium Red Pepper
1/2 cup Cooked Thin Spaghetti
3 Tbsp Reduced Sodium Chicken Broth
1 tsp Sesame Oil

Instructions:

Slice tenderloin and marinate with soy sauce, garlic, ginger, and red pepper flakes for 20 minutes.

Preheat Blackstone griddle to medium-high.

Stir-fry pork for 4-5 minutes, then add peas and red pepper.

Add noodles and broth, cook for another minute.

Stir in sesame oil and serve.

Nutrition Facts (1 portion):

Energy: 367 Kcal
Carbs: 42g
Proteins: 35g
Fats: 5.59g

Pork Jerky

Portion Size: 2
Duration: 30 min

Ingredients:

8 3/4 oz Pork Mince
1 Tbsp Fish Sauce
2 Tbsps. Rose Wine
1 Tbsp Soy Sauce
1/2 Tbsp Dark Soy Sauce
1/4 cup Sugar

Instructions:

Mix ingredients with pork mince and refrigerate for 2 hours.

Flatten mince on foil with a plastic sheet.

Preheat Blackstone griddle to 300°F.

Grill meat for 12 minutes, remove gravy, switch to high heat.

Grill for 8-10 minutes until charred. Cool and slice.

Nutrition Facts (1 portion):

Energy: 242 Kcal
Carbs: 16g
Proteins: 27g
Fats: 7.5g

Pork Loin Stuffed with Spinach

Portion Size: 2
Duration: 150 min

Ingredients:

1/5 Container Thawed, Drained Frozen Chopped Spinach
1/4 cup Margarine
1/8 cup Dry Bread Crumbs
1/5 cup Sliced Onion
1/4 lb Pork Tenderloin
4/5 tbsp. Ketchup
4/5 tbsp. Teriyaki Sauce

1/5 tsp Ground Cumin

1 Garlic Clove

Instructions:

Sauté spinach, butter, onions, and garlic.

Cut tenderloin, stuff with spinach mixture.

Combine teriyaki sauce and ketchup.

Baste tenderloin and season with cumin.

Roast on Blackstone griddle at 350°F for 2 hours.

Nutrition Facts (1 portion):

Energy: 432 Kcal

Carbs: 12g

Proteins: 59g

Fats: 14g

Pork Chop with Creamy Mushroom Sauce

Portion Size: 2

Duration: 30 min

Ingredients:

2 Bone-in Pork Chops, 1 lb

Salt & Pepper

1 1/2 tsp Olive Oil

1/4 cup Shallots, Minced

4 oz Mixed Mushrooms, Sliced

1/4 cup Dry White Wine

1/4 cup Fresh Parsley, Minced

Instructions:

Season pork chops and cook on Blackstone griddle with oil.

Cook for 5-7 minutes each side.

Sauté shallots and mushrooms, add wine.

Simmer with herbs and serve with chops.

Nutrition Facts (1 portion):

Energy: 357 Kcal

Carbs: 6g

Proteins: 29g

Fats: 22g

Pork and Green Bean Stir-Fry

Portion Size: 2

Duration: 30 min

Ingredients:

1/8 cup Apricot Jam

1 Tbsp Low Sodium Soy Sauce

1/2 Tbsp Sesame Oil

2 tsp Garlic-Chile Sauce

1/2 lb Pork Tenderloin, Sliced

1/8 cup Cornstarch

1 1/2 tsp Grapeseed or Avocado Oil

6 oz Green Beans, Trimmed

1/4 cup Scallions, Sliced

Instructions:

Mix jam, soy sauce, sesame oil, and chili-garlic sauce.

Coat pork with cornstarch.

Stir-fry pork on Blackstone griddle, add green beans.

Add jam mixture and scallions, serve.

Nutrition Facts (1 portion):

Energy: 387 Kcal

Carbs: 29g

Proteins: 27g

Fats: 19g

Pork Butt Roast with Vegetable

Portion Size: 2
Duration: 70 min

Ingredients:

Salt, Pepper, Garlic Powder

1 1/2 lbs. Pork Butt Roast

5 Potatoes

4 Carrots

1/2 Onion

1/2 cup Mushrooms

Instructions:

Season pork with spices and brown on Blackstone griddle.

Place in a griddle-safe baking dish, add onion, water, and bake.

Add vegetables, bake for 1 hour.

Rest before serving.

Nutrition Facts (1 portion):

Energy: 690 Kcal

Carbs: 80g

Proteins: 73g

Fats: 20g

Pork Fried Rice

Portion Size: 2
Duration: 40 min

Ingredients:

1/4 lb Pork Tenderloin, Chopped

1 Tbsp Peanut Oil

1/3 Large White Onion, Chopped

1/3 cup Young Peas

1/3 cup Baby Carrots, Chopped

1/10 tsp Crushed Red Chili Flakes

1 cup Soy Sauce

1 cup Cooked Rice

Instructions:

Heat Blackstone griddle, add oil.

Cook pork, then add onion.

Add peas, carrots, soy sauce, and chili flakes.

Stir in rice, cook until done.

Nutrition Facts (1 portion):

Energy: 603 Kcal

Carbs: 108g

Proteins: 20g

Fats: 8.1g

Poultry

Brown Rice, Leek, and Stir-Fried Chicken

Portion Size: 2
Duration: 55 min

Ingredients:
1/2 tbsp Olive Oil
150g Chicken Breast, Sliced
50g Chorizo, Chopped
1 Leek, Sliced
1/2 Red Pepper, Crushed
40g Kale, Chopped
1/2 tbsp Low Salt Soy Sauce
1/2 tbsp Vinegar
250g Wholegrain Rice

Instructions:
Preheat Blackstone griddle to medium-high. Cook chicken in olive oil for 3 minutes.
Add chorizo, cook until browned.
Sauté leek and red pepper, then kale.
Add rice, soy sauce, and vinegar. Combine with chicken and chorizo.
Heat for 3 minutes and serve.

Nutrition Facts (1 portion):
Energy: 398 Kcal
Carbs: 33g
Proteins: 26g
Fats: 16g

Baked Parmesan Cheese Chicken

Portion Size: 2
Duration: 35 min

Ingredients:
1 cup Shredded Parmesan Cheese
1/2 tsp Garlic Powder
1 tsp Celery Salt
1 tsp Cayenne Pepper
6 oz Chicken Thighs, Skinless, Boneless

Instructions:
Preheat Blackstone griddle to 370°F.
Mix cheese, celery salt, pepper, and garlic powder.
Coat chicken in olive oil, then in cheese mixture.
Cook on griddle until internal temperature reaches 165°F.

Nutrition Facts (1 portion):
Energy: 300 Kcal
Carbs: 1g
Proteins: 28g
Fats: 22g

Chicken Vegetable Stew

Portion Size: 2
Duration: 35 min

Ingredients:
120g Chicken Breasts
1 cup Chicken Broth
1 Potato, Cubed
1/2 Onion, Diced
1 Garlic Clove, Minced
1 Carrot, Diced
1/4 tsp Dried Oregano
1/4 tsp Fresh Dill
1 Celery Stalk
Salt, Pepper

1 tbsp Olive Oil

Instructions:

Sauté vegetables in olive oil on Blackstone griddle.

Add chicken, broth, and spices.

Cook until chicken is done and potatoes are soft.

Garnish with dill and serve.

Nutrition Facts (1 portion):

Energy: 775 Kcal

Carbs: 23g

Proteins: 32g

Fats: 62g

Chicken Curry

Portion Size: 2

Duration: 45 min

Ingredients:

1/2 lb Chicken Breast

3/8 cup Fat-Free Evaporated Milk

1 Garlic Clove, Minced

1/2 cup Mushrooms, Chopped

1/2 cup Chicken Bisque

1 Carrot, Sliced

1/8 large Onion, Chopped

1/4 tsp Curry Powder

1/2 tsp Cornstarch

1/2 tbsp Water

Instructions:

Cook chicken on Blackstone griddle until done.

Mix chicken, bisque, milk, curry, garlic, mushrooms, onion, and carrot in a pot. Bring to boil.

Mix cornstarch with water, add to pot. Thicken sauce.

Serve with rice.

Nutrition Facts (1 portion):

Energy: 183 Kcal

Carbs: 11g

Proteins: 27g

Fats: 3.4g

Chicken Rice

Portion Size: 2

Duration: 25 min

Ingredients:

1 cup Water

1 cup Asparagus, Cut

1/2 Rice Blend Pack

1/8 cup Low-Fat Butter

3/8 lb Chicken Breast, Sliced

1/2 tsp Minced Garlic

1/2 Carrot, Shredded

1 tbsp Lime Juice

Instructions:

Cook rice, asparagus, and butter in a pot until water is absorbed.

Cook chicken, garlic, and carrot on Blackstone griddle.

Mix cooked chicken and vegetables with rice.

Add lime juice and serve.

Nutrition Facts (1 portion):

Energy: 324 Kcal

Carbs: 23g

Proteins: 28g

Fats: 15g

Lemon Herb Roast Chicken

Portion Size*:* 2
Duration*:* 15 min

Ingredients*:*
1/3 Lemon
1/3 can Cream of Chicken Soup
1/3 tbsp Fresh Rosemary
1/3 tbsp Fresh Thyme
1 Garlic Clove, Minced
1/3 Roasting Chicken
1/10 cup Dry White Wine
1/10 cup Water

Instructions*:*
Mix soup, herbs, garlic, lemon juice, and zest.
Set aside 1 cup soup mixture for gravy. Rub remaining mixture on chicken.
Roast chicken on Blackstone griddle. Baste with soup mixture.
Make gravy with pan juices, wine, and reserved soup mixture.
Serve chicken with gravy.

Nutrition Facts (1 portion)*:*
Energy: 112 Kcal
Carbs: 2.57g
Proteins: 13g
Fats: 3.82g

Chicken Bhuna Masala on Griddle

Portion Size*:* 2
Duration*:* 35 min

Ingredients*:*
1 tsp. Cumin Seeds
1 tsp. Coriander Seeds

1 Tbsp Vegetable Oil
1 Chicken Breast, Cubed
1/2 Cinnamon Stick
2 Tomatoes, Diced
1/2 Red Onion
2 Garlic Cloves
1 tsp Fresh Ginger, Chopped
1 tsp Curry Powder
1 tsp Chili Powder
1/3 cup Coconut Milk
1/3 cup White Wine
1 cup Cooked Basmati Rice

Instructions*:*
Toast cumin and coriander seeds on the Blackstone griddle. Grind them.
Cook chicken in oil, season with salt and pepper.
Add ground spices, white wine, tomatoes, onion, garlic, ginger, chili powder, curry powder, cinnamon, and coconut milk.
Bring to boil, then simmer to thicken.
Serve with basmati rice.

Nutrition Facts (1 portion)*:*
Energy: 464.1 Kcal
Carbs: 66g
Proteins: 8.4g
Fats: 19g

Chicken Protein Pots

Portion Size*:* 2
Duration*:* 35 min

Ingredients*:*
1/4 cup Carrots
2 tsp Butter

1/4 cup Sweet Peas

1 Egg, Beaten

1/2 tsp Garlic Powder

1/4 lb Chicken Breast, Cooked and Chopped

1/2 Onion, Chopped

2 tbsp Soy Sauce

Dash of Salt and Pepper

Instructions:

Melt butter on the griddle. Sauté carrots, peas, and onions.

Push veggies to the side, scramble eggs.

Mix veggies and eggs, add garlic powder and soy sauce.

Stir in chicken and rice. Cook until heated.

Season with salt and pepper, garnish with green onions.

Nutrition Facts (1 portion):

Energy: 162 Kcal

Carbs: 6.7g

Proteins: 16g

Fats: 8.4g

Air Fried Chicken General Tso's Burger

Portion Size: 2
Duration: 35 min

Ingredients:

1 Small Egg

1/2 lb Chicken Thighs, Boneless, Skinless

1/4 cup Cornstarch

1/8 tsp Salt & White Pepper

3 Tbsp Low-Salt Chicken Broth

1 tbsp Soy Sauce

1 tbsp Ketchup

1 tsp Sugar

1 Tbsp Rice Vinegar

1/2 Tbsp Canola Oil

1 tsp Garlic and Ginger, Chopped

2 tbsp Green Onion, Sliced

1 tsp Toasted Sesame Oil

Instructions:

Whisk egg and coat chicken. Mix with cornstarch, salt, and pepper.

Cook chicken on preheated Blackstone griddle until crispy.

Make sauce: broth, soy sauce, ketchup, sugar, and vinegar. Cook garlic and ginger in oil, add sauce.

Add chicken to sauce, cook together. Add sesame oil.

Serve with green onions.

Nutrition Facts (1 portion):

Energy: 302 Kcal

Carbs: 18g

Proteins: 26g

Fats: 13g

Chicken Club Wraps

Portion Size: 2
Duration: 35 min

Ingredients:

1/2 lb Chicken Breast, Sliced

1/4 tsp Pepper

3 Tbsp Greek Yogurt

3 Tbsp Cider Vinegar

3 tsp Onion, Minced

1 tbsp Olive Oil

1/2 Tomato, Diced

1/2 Avocado, Chopped

4 Green Leaf Lettuce Leaves

2 Whole Wheat Tortillas

Instructions:

Cook chicken on Blackstone griddle, season with pepper.

Mix yogurt, vinegar, onion, oil, tomato, avocado, and chicken.

Spread on tortillas, add lettuce.

Roll and serve.

Nutrition Facts (1 portion):

Energy: 526 Kcal

Carbs: 39g

Proteins: 34g

Fats: 26g

Chicken Stew in Skillet

Portion Size: 2

Duration: 35 min

Ingredients:

1/6 cup Flour

3/4 lb Chicken Breasts

Salt and Pepper to Taste

1 1/2 Tbsp Butter

1/2 Garlic Clove, Minced

1 1/2 Potatoes & Carrots, Sliced

1/2 Onion, Sliced

1 can Chicken Broth

1 1/2 Tbsp Flour

Instructions:

Coat chicken in flour, salt, and pepper.

Cook chicken in butter on griddle.

Add onions, garlic, carrots, and potatoes.

Add broth, bring to boil, simmer 30 min.

Serve stew.

Nutrition Facts (1 portion):

Energy: 516 Kcal

Carbs: 50g

Proteins: 40g

Fats: 17g

Chicken Shashlik

Portion Size: 2

Duration: 120 min

Ingredients:

250g Chicken Breast Fillets, Sliced

Salt

1/2 tsp Garlic and Ginger, Chopped

1/2 tsp Cumin, Turmeric, Chili Powder

1 tbsp Olive Oil

1 Small Onion, Sliced

1 Medium Capsicum, Sliced

1/4 tsp Chat Masala

2 tbsp Yogurt

Instructions:

Marinate chicken in spices and yogurt.

Cook chicken in oil on Blackstone griddle until tender.

Sauté onions and capsicum in oil.

Combine with cooked chicken.

Nutrition Facts (1 portion):

Energy: 421 Kcal

Carbs: 27g

Proteins: 21g

Fats: 27.5g

Fried Chicken

Portion Size*: 2*
Duration*: 30 min*

Ingredients*:*

1 cup Chicken, Cut

1/4 cup Whole Wheat Bread Crumbs

1 tbsp Salt

1/2 tbsp Paprika

1/4 tbsp Pepper

1/4 cup Butter or Olive Oil

Instructions*:*

Mix breadcrumbs, salt, paprika, and pepper.

Coat chicken in butter or oil, then in breadcrumb mix.

Cook on Blackstone griddle until tender.

Serve with salsa or mint sauce.

Nutrition Facts (1 portion):

Energy: 453 Kcal

Carbs: 35g

Proteins: 70g

Fats: 16g

Crispy Skinned Baked Chicken Drumstick

Portion Size*: 2*
Duration*: 55 min*

Ingredients*:*

8 (120g each) Skin-on Chicken Drumsticks

2 tbsp Olive Oil

1 tsp Kosher Salt

½ tsp Black Pepper

1 tsp Garlic Powder

1 tsp Onion Powder

1 tsp Smoked Paprika

¼ tsp Cayenne Pepper

Instructions*:*

Preheat Blackstone griddle to medium-high heat.

Combine olive oil, salt, pepper, garlic, onion powder, smoked paprika, and cayenne pepper. Coat drumsticks evenly.

Place drumsticks on the griddle. Cook for about 40 minutes, turning occasionally, until internal temperature reaches 165°F.

Serve hot with favorite sides.

Nutrition Facts (1 portion):

Energy: 288 Kcal

Carbs: 10g

Proteins: 28g

Fats: 18g

Pon Pon Chicken

Portion Size*: 2*
Duration*: 25 min*

Ingredients*:*

2 Boneless Chicken Breasts

4 Cucumber Slices

1 Tbsp Salt

2 Tbsp Sesame Seed Paste or 1 Tbsp Oil

5 Tbsp Soy Sauce

3 tsp Sugar

2 Tbsp Vinegar

3 Tbsp Worcestershire Sauce

1/2 tsp Garlic & Ginger Juice

2 Dashes Black Pepper

1 tsp Corn Flour

Instructions*:*

Cook chicken on the Blackstone griddle until done. Cool and slice.

Mix cucumbers with salt, drain, and set on a dish.

Prepare dressing in a pan with water, sugar, soy sauce, vinegar, Worcestershire sauce, and corn flour. Bring to a simmer.

Serve chicken over cucumbers and top with dressing.

Nutrition Facts (1 portion):
Energy: 444 Kcal
Carbs: 21g
Proteins: 59g
Fats: 15g

Thai Chicken Curry

Portion Size: 2
Duration: 25 min

Ingredients:
1 tbsp Vegetable Oil
1/2 tsp Curry Paste
5/8 lb Chicken Breast, Cut-up
1/2 Onion, Chopped
1/2 Red Bell Pepper, Sliced
1/2 cup Light Coconut Milk
1/2 tbsp Lemon Zest
1/2 tbsp Fish Sauce
1/2 tbsp Lime Juice
1/6 cup Fresh Cilantro, Finely Chopped

Instructions:
Heat oil on the griddle. Sauté curry paste.

Add chicken, bell pepper, onion, and cook until chicken is done.

Stir in coconut milk, lemon zest, fish sauce, and lime juice.

Add cilantro and serve hot.

Nutrition Facts (1 portion):
Energy: 343 Kcal
Carbs: 8.3g
Proteins: 30g
Fats: 22g

Baked Salsa Chicken

Portion Size: 2
Duration: 85 min

Ingredients:
3/4 cup Tomatoes
1/4 cup Onions
3/4 tbsp Garlic
1/2 cup Avocado
1/8 cup Lime Juice
Salt and Pepper
1/4 lb Chicken Breast
1/2 cup Long-Grain Rice
1 cup Chicken Broth

Instructions:
Preheat Blackstone griddle to medium heat.

Mix tomatoes, onions, garlic, avocado, and lime juice. Season with salt and pepper.

Spread rice on the griddle, top with chicken breast.

Pour chicken broth over the rice and chicken.

Top with salsa mix and cover with foil.

Cook for 1 hour, checking occasionally.

Nutrition Facts (1 portion):
Energy: 173 Kcal
Carbs: 24g

Proteins: 14g

Fats: 19g

Roast Chicken Breast with Garbanzo Beans

Portion Size: 2

Duration: 35 min

Ingredients:

1/8 cup Olive Oil

2 Garlic Cloves, Squeezed

1/2 tbsp Smoked Paprika

1/2 tsp Ground Cumin

1/4 tsp Dried Red Pepper, Crushed

1/4 cup Plain Yogurt

2 Chicken Breast Halves

8 oz Garbanzo Beans (Chickpeas), Drained

6.5 oz Cherry Tomatoes

1/2 cup Fresh Cilantro, Chopped

Instructions:

Preheat Blackstone griddle to high heat.

Mix olive oil, garlic, paprika, cumin, and red pepper. Set aside some for yogurt sauce.

Cook chicken on the griddle with some spicy oil mixture.

Mix beans, tomatoes, and cilantro with remaining oil. Spread around chicken.

Cook until chicken is done, top with cilantro.

Nutrition Facts (1 portion):

Energy: 364 Kcal

Carbs: 33g

Proteins: 12g

Fats: 21g

Grilled Chicken with White BBQ Sauce

Portion Size: 2

Duration: 35 min

Ingredients:

1 lb Chicken Parts

Parsley Leaves for Garnish

White BBQ Sauce (made with horseradish, lemon juice, vinegar, sugar, mayonnaise, cayenne pepper)

Instructions:

Preheat griddle to medium-low.

Season and cook chicken.

Prepare White BBQ Sauce, apply to chicken during cooking.

Serve chicken garnished with parsley and extra sauce.

Nutrition Facts (1 portion):

Energy: 374 Kcal

Carbs: 15g

Proteins: 30g

Fats: 28g

Chicken Quinoa Bowl with Olives and Cucumber

Portion Size: 2

Duration: 35 min

Ingredients:

Salt

1 cup Quinoa

Ground Pepper

1/8 cup Slivered Almonds

1/6 tsp Paprika

3oz Red Pepper, Roasted

1/8cup Kalamata Olives

2 tbsp Olive Oil

1/8 cup Red Onion

1/2 Cucumber, Diced

1/8 cup Mozzarella Cheese

1 Tbsp Parsley

Instructions:

Preheat griddle, cook chicken seasoned with salt and pepper.

In a bowl, mix quinoa, olives, onion, almonds, oil, and spices.

Serve quinoa topped with chicken, cucumber, cheese, and parsley.

Nutrition Facts (1 portion):

Energy: 481 Kcal

Carbs: 31g

Proteins: 34g

Fats: 27g

Chicken Quinoa Casserole

Portion Size: 2

Duration: 35 min

Ingredients:

½ clove Garlic, minced

1 cup Chicken, cooked & cubed

1/3 cup Quinoa

3 oz. Mushrooms, sliced

1/3 tbsp. Olive Oil

7 oz. Black Beans, drained

Spices (e.g., Paprika, Black Pepper) to taste

Instructions:

Pre-cook quinoa as per package

instructions.

Preheat the Blackstone griddle to medium heat.

Sauté garlic in olive oil until fragrant.

Add chicken, mushrooms, and black beans to the griddle. Season with spices.

Combine cooked quinoa with chicken mixture on the griddle.

Stir everything well and heat through.

Serve warm directly from the griddle.

Nutrition Facts (1 portion):

Energy: 256 Kcal

Carbs: 16g

Proteins: 21g

Fats: 12g

Baked Chicken Tenders

Portion Size: 2

Duration: 35 min

Ingredients:

2 Chicken Breast Halves, skinless & boneless

1 Egg White, lightly beaten

1/2 tbsp. Water

1/2 tsp Lemon Peel, finely shredded

1/4 cup Breadcrumbs, seasoned

1/8 cup Parmesan Cheese, finely shredded

Instructions:

Preheat the Blackstone griddle to 400°F.

Mix egg white, water, and lemon peel in a bowl. In another bowl, combine breadcrumbs and Parmesan cheese.

Dip chicken strips in the egg mixture, then coat with breadcrumb mixture.

Place coated chicken strips on the griddle. Cook for about 15 minutes or until no longer pink (165°F internal temperature).

Serve with your favorite dipping sauce.

Nutrition Facts (1 portion):
Energy: 207 Kcal
Carbs: 11g
Proteins: 32g
Fats: 3g

Chicken Quesadilla

Portion Size: 2
Duration: 35 min

Ingredients:
2 Chicken Breasts, cooked & chopped
2/5 Onion, diced
1/3 can Green Chilies
1/3 packet Taco Seasoning Mix
Salsa & Cheese to taste
2 Tortillas

Instructions:
Preheat Blackstone griddle to medium heat.

Sauté chicken and onion until browned. Add green chilies and taco seasoning mix. Stir in some salsa.

Place tortillas on the griddle. Fill one half with chicken mixture and cheese. Fold over to close.

Cook until tortillas are crispy and cheese is melted, flipping once.

Slice and serve hot.

Nutrition Facts (1 portion):
Energy: 53 Kcal
Carbs: 5.4g
Proteins: 2.3g

Fats: 2.4g

Chicken Jalfrezi

Portion Size: 2
Duration: 65 min

Ingredients:
2/3 tbsp. Vegetable Oil
1/3 Onion, sliced
2/3 cloves Garlic, minced
1/2 lb. Chicken Thighs, boneless & skinless, cut in half
1 tsp Turmeric
1/3 tsp Chili Powder
1/2 tsp Salt
1/3 can Tomatoes, peeled & sliced
2/3 tbsp. Butter
1 tsp Cumin, ground
1 tsp Coriander, powdered
2/3 tbsp. Ginger, grated

Instructions:
Heat oil on Blackstone griddle over medium-high heat.

Sauté onions and garlic until golden. Add chicken, turmeric, chili powder, and salt. Cook until chicken is browned.

Add tomatoes, butter, ginger, cumin, and coriander. Mix well.

Reduce heat and simmer until chicken is cooked through and sauce thickens.

Serve hot with rice or naan.

Nutrition Facts (1 portion):
Energy: 602 Kcal
Carbs: 5.18g
Proteins: 12g

Fats: 56g

Chicken Patties with Mashed Potato

Portion Size: 2
Duration: 35 min

Ingredients:
170g Chicken Breast, hand-chopped
1 ½ tbsp. Parsley, chopped
1 Spring Onion, chopped
½ tsp Butter
20g Breadcrumbs
Salt and Pepper to taste
For The Swede and Potato Mash:
1 medium Potato, boiled
¼ cup Swede, boiled
30g Cheddar Cheese, grated
1 Garlic Clove, finely chopped

Instructions:
Preheat Blackstone griddle to medium heat.

Sauté spring onion in butter until soft. Cool and mix with chicken, parsley, breadcrumbs, salt, and pepper.

Form mixture into patties and cook on griddle until browned on both sides.

For mash: Mash boiled potato and swede together. Stir in garlic, cheese, and season to taste.

Serve chicken patties with mashed potato and swede.

Nutrition Facts (1 portion):
Energy: 364 Kcal
Carbs: 33g
Proteins: 34g
Fats: 10.6g

Beef

Black Bean and Beef Tostadas

Portion Size: 2
Duration: 30 min

Ingredients:
1/4-pound Lean Ground Beef
1/2 can Black Beans, rinsed
1/2 can Diced Tomatoes and Green Chiles
1/2 can Refried Beans, warmed
4 Tostada Shells

Instructions:
Preheat the Blackstone griddle over medium heat.

Cook ground beef on the griddle for 4-6 min, crumbling it as it cooks.

Add tomatoes and simmer until liquid nearly evaporates (6-8 min).

Stir in black beans and heat through.

Spread refried beans on tostada shells.

Top with beef mixture and preferred garnishes.

Nutrition Facts (1 portion):
Energy: 392 Kcal
Carbs: 46g
Proteins: 23g
Fats: 14g

Tomato Hamburger Soup

Portion Size: 2
Duration: 4 hrs.

Ingredients:
7.6 oz V8 Juice

5 oz Frozen Mixed Vegetables
0.16-pound Ground Beef, cooked & drained
1.6 oz Cream of Mushroom Soup, condensed
1/2 tsp Dried Minced Onion
Pepper and Salt to taste

Instructions:
Preheat Blackstone griddle to low heat.

Combine all ingredients except seasoning in a pot on the griddle.

Cook with the lid on for 4-5 hrs or until heated thoroughly.

Season with pepper and salt as desired.

Nutrition Facts (1 portion):
Energy: 125 Kcal
Carbs: 9g
Proteins: 12g
Fats: 5g

Burger Americana

Portion Size: 2
Duration: 25 min

Ingredients:
¼ cup Seasoned Bread Crumbs
1/2 Large Egg, lightly beaten
¼ tsp Salt
¼ tsp Pepper
½ pound Ground Beef
½ Tbsp Olive Oil
2 Sesame Seed Hamburger Buns
Toppings

Instructions:
Preheat Blackstone griddle to medium heat.

In a bowl, mix egg, bread crumbs, salt, and pepper. Add ground beef; mix gently.

Form into 2 patties, pressing a thumbprint in the center.

Brush patties with oil and cook on the griddle until an internal temperature of 160°F is reached.

Serve on buns with desired toppings.

Nutrition Facts (1 portion):

Energy: 429 Kcal

Carbs: 32g

Proteins: 28g

Fats: 20g

Asian Beef and Noodles

Portion Size: 2

Duration: 20 min

Ingredients:

½ pound Lean Ground Beef

1 package Soy Sauce Ramen Noodles, crumbled

1 cup Water

1 cup Frozen Broccoli Stir-Fry Vegetable Blend

1/8 tsp Ginger, minced

1 Tbsp Green Onion, sliced

Instructions:

Preheat the Blackstone griddle to medium heat.

Cook ground beef until no longer pink, breaking it up.

Stir in one packet of ramen seasoning until dissolved.

In a skillet, add water, vegetables, ginger, noodles, and remaining seasoning. Boil, then simmer until noodles are tender.

Return beef to the skillet, stirring in green onion.

Serve hot.

Nutrition Facts (1 portion):

Energy: 383 Kcal

Carbs: 29g

Proteins: 27g

Fats: 16g

Smothered Burritos

Portion Size: 2

Duration: 30 min

Ingredients:

½ can Green Enchilada Sauce

½ cup Salsa Verde

½ pound Ground Beef

2 Flour Tortillas (10 inches)

1 cup Cheddar Cheese, shredded

Instructions:

Preheat Blackstone griddle to medium heat.

In a bowl, mix salsa verde and enchilada sauce.

Cook ground beef on griddle until browned; drain.

Stir in half of the sauce mixture into the beef.

Spread 2/3 cup beef mix and 3 tbsp cheese on each tortilla, fold and place on a greased griddle pan.

Top with remaining sauce and cheese. Cook until cheese melts.

Nutrition Facts (1 portion):

Energy: 624 Kcal

Carbs: 44g

Proteins: 36g

Fats: 33g

Beef and Broccoli

Portion Size: 2
Duration: 15 min

Ingredients:
8 oz. Flank Steak, thinly sliced
2 cups Broccoli Florets
1 tbsp. Vegetable Oil
1 tbsp. Soy Sauce
1 tsp. Cornstarch
1 tbsp. Oyster Sauce
Salt and Pepper, to taste
1/4 tsp. Garlic Powder

Instructions:
Preheat Blackstone griddle to medium-high heat.

In a bowl, mix garlic powder, cornstarch, sauces, and seasonings.

Cook sliced beef in oil until browned, then add broccoli and cook until tender.

Add soy sauce mixture, stirring to coat evenly.
Serve with rice.

Nutrition Facts (1 portion):
Energy: 305 Kcal
Carbs: 14g
Proteins: 33g
Fats: 13g

Slow Cooker Beef Stew

Portion Size: 2
Duration: 4 hrs.

Ingredients:
1 lb. Beef Stew Meat
2 cups Mixed Vegetables, chopped
1 can Diced Tomatoes, undrained
1 cup Beef Broth
1 tbsp. Worcestershire Sauce
Salt and Pepper, to taste

Instructions:
Place beef stew meat, vegetables, broth, Worcestershire sauce, and tomatoes in a pot on the Blackstone griddle.

Cook with the lid on over low heat for 4-5 hrs or until beef and vegetables are tender.
Serve hot.

Nutrition Facts (1 portion):
Energy: 337 Kcal
Carbs: 31g
Proteins: 33g
Fats: 9g

Beef and Vegetable Soup

Portion Size: 2
Duration: 35 min

Ingredients:
8 oz. Beef Stew Meat
2 Cloves Garlic, minced
2 cups Mixed Vegetables (Carrots, Celery, Potatoes)
4 cups Beef Broth
1 Onion, chopped
Pepper and Salt

Instructions:
Preheat the Blackstone griddle to medium heat.

Brown beef stew meat with garlic and onion until thoroughly cooked (about 5 mins).

Add mixed vegetables and beef broth to the griddle.

Bring to a boil, then simmer until vegetables are cooked (about 20 mins).

Season with pepper and salt. Serve warm.

Nutrition Facts (1 portion):
Energy: 236 Kcal
Carbs: 8g
Proteins: 22g
Fats: 8g

Beef and Guinness Stew

Portion Size: 2
Duration: 2-3 hrs.

Ingredients:
1 lb. Beef Stew Meat
2 Cloves Garlic, minced
2 Celery Stalks, chopped
1 Onion, chopped
1/2 cup Guinness Beer
2 Carrots, chopped
1 cup Beef Broth
1 Bay Leaf
1 tbsp. Tomato Paste
1 tsp. Dried Thyme
Pepper and Salt

Instructions:
Preheat Blackstone griddle to medium-high heat.

Brown beef with onion and garlic (5-7 mins).

Add carrots and celery, cook until slightly softened.

Stir in Guinness, beef broth, and remaining ingredients.

Simmer for 1-2 hrs until meat is tender and flavors blend.

Serve hot.

Nutrition Facts (1 portion):
Energy: 397 Kcal
Carbs: 17g
Proteins: 42g
Fats: 14g

Beef and Sweet Potato Curry

Portion Size: 2
Duration: 30 min

Ingredients:
1 lb. Beef Sirloin, thinly sliced
1 Onion, chopped
1 Sweet Potato, peeled & chopped
1 can (14 oz.) Coconut Milk
2 Cloves Garlic, minced
1 tbsp. Curry Powder
Pepper and Salt

Instructions:
Cook beef, onion, and garlic on the griddle until browned.

Remove beef, add sweet potato, and cook until starting to soften.

Stir in coconut milk, curry powder, salt, and pepper.

Return beef to the griddle and simmer until sweet potato is cooked.

Serve hot.

Nutrition Facts (1 portion):
Energy: 541 Kcal

Carbs: 22g

Proteins: 35g

Fats: 35g

Beef and Spinach Lasagna

Portion Size: 2

Duration: 30 min

Ingredients:

4 Lasagna Noodles

1/2 lb. Ground Beef

1/2 cup Marinara Sauce

1/2 cup Ricotta Cheese

1/2 cup Shredded Mozzarella Cheese

1 cup Spinach, chopped

Pepper and Salt

Instructions:

Preheat the Blackstone griddle and cook ground beef.

Combine marinara sauce and cooked beef.

Mix ricotta, mozzarella, spinach, salt, and pepper.

Layer meat sauce, noodles, and cheese mixture in a baking dish.

Bake until cheese is bubbly (20 min).

Nutrition Facts (1 portion):

Energy: 468 Kcal

Carbs: 37g

Proteins: 29g

Fats: 21g

Beef and Cabbage Soup

Portion Size: 2

Duration: 25 min

Ingredients:

1/2 lb. Ground Beef

2 cups Beef Broth

1 cup Water

1 cup Chopped Cabbage

1/2 cup Chopped Carrot

1/2 cup Chopped Celery

1/2 cup Chopped Onion

1 Clove Garlic, minced

1 Bay Leaf

Pepper and Salt

Instructions:

Brown ground beef on the griddle, drain fat.

Add broth, water, cabbage, carrot, celery, onion, garlic, and seasonings.

Simmer until vegetables are tender (20 mins).

Serve hot after removing the bay leaf.

Nutrition Facts (1 portion):

Energy: 191 Kcal

Carbs: 8g

Proteins: 15g

Fats: 11g

Beef and Cheese Quesadillas

Portion Size: 2

Duration: 15 min

Ingredients:

2 Flour Tortillas

1/2 lb. Ground Beef

1/2 cup Shredded Cheddar Cheese

1/2 cup Salsa

Pepper and Salt

Instructions:

Cook ground beef on the griddle, season with salt and pepper.

Lay tortillas, add beef, cheese, and salsa.

Top with another tortilla and cook until cheese melts.

Cut into quarters and serve.

Nutrition Facts (1 portion):

Energy: 459 Kcal

Carbs: 28g

Proteins: 30g

Fats: 24g

Ravioli Lasagna

Portion Size: 2

Duration: 65 min

Ingredients:

1/4 lb. Ground Beef

¼ Jar (28 oz) Spaghetti Sauce

6 oz Frozen Sausage or Cheese Ravioli

¼ Cups Shredded Part-Skim Mozzarella Cheese

Minced Fresh Basil (Optional)

Instructions:

Preheat Blackstone griddle to medium heat.

Cook and crumble the beef on the griddle for 5-7 minutes; drain.

Place 1/3 of the spaghetti sauce in a heat-resistant dish on the griddle. Layer with 1/2 of the beef and ravioli, then 1/2 cup of cheese. Repeat layers.

Add remaining sauce and cheese on top.

Cover and cook for 40-45 mins until thoroughly heated. Use a lid or aluminum foil to cover.

Serve with basil on top, if preferred.

Nutrition Facts (1 portion):

Energy: 438 Kcal

Carbs: 42g

Proteins: 26g

Fats: 18g

Mexican Stuffed Peppers

Portion Size: 2

Duration: 30 min

Ingredients:

1/4-pound Lean Ground Beef

1/4 Envelope Mexican-Style Rice and Pasta Mix

1/4 Cups Water

2 Medium Sweet Peppers

1/4 Can Diced Tomatoes and Green Chiles, Undrained

1/2 Cup Shredded Mexican Cheese Blend, Divided

Minced Fresh Cilantro

Instructions:

Preheat the Blackstone griddle to medium heat.

Cook and crumble the beef for 5-7 minutes; drain.

Stir in tomatoes, rice mixture, and water. Bring to a boil then simmer for 6-8 mins.

Cut tops off peppers and remove seeds.

Place peppers on the griddle. Fill each with 1/3 cup of the meat mixture, add 2 tsps. of cheese.

Cook covered for 25 minutes. Add remaining cheese and cook uncovered for 5-10 mins.

Garnish with cilantro.

Nutrition Facts (1 portion):
Energy: 301 Kcal
Carbs: 23g
Proteins: 20g
Fats: 14g

Pizza Roll-Ups

Portion Size: 2
Duration: 35 min

Ingredients:
¼ Pound Ground Beef
½ Can Tomato Sauce
¼ Tsp Dried Oregano
1 Tube Refrigerated Crescent Rolls
¼ Cup Shredded Part-Skim Mozzarella Cheese

Instructions:
Cook beef on the griddle, drain off the fat.

Stir in mozzarella cheese, oregano, and tomato sauce.

Form crescent dough into rectangles. Spread the meat mixture along one side.

Roll up the dough, slice into pieces, and place on the griddle.

Cook for 15 mins at 375°F using a griddle cover or lid.

Nutrition Facts (1 portion):

Energy: 94 Kcal
Carbs: 9g
Proteins: 4g
Fats: 5g

Beefy Tortellini Skillet

Portion Size: 2
Duration: 20 min

Ingredients:
½ Pound Ground Beef
¼ Tsp Montreal Steak Seasoning
½ Cup Water
½ Tsp Beef Bouillon Granules
½ Package (8 oz) Frozen Cheese Tortellini
½ Cup Shredded Italian Cheese Blend

Instructions:
Preheat the Blackstone griddle to medium heat.

Sauté beef until cooked, about 5-6 mins. Season with steak spice.

Dissolve bouillon in water and add to the griddle.

Stir in tortellini, cover and cook for 3-4 mins.

Top with cheese until melted.

Nutrition Facts (1 portion):
Energy: 566 Kcal
Carbs: 37g
Proteins: 39g
Fats: 28g

Super Spaghetti Sauce

Portion Size: 2
Duration: 30 min

Ingredients:

½ Lb. Ground Beef

½ Lb. Smoked Kielbasa, Sliced

1 Jar (12 oz) Spaghetti Sauce with Mushrooms

½ Jar (8 oz) Chunky Salsa

Hot Cooked Pasta

Instructions:

Cook beef on the Blackstone griddle, then set aside.

Cook kielbasa for 5-6 mins.

Add spaghetti sauce, salsa, and beef; heat thoroughly.

Serve alongside pasta.

Nutrition Facts (1 portion):

Energy: 325 Kcal

Carbs: 18g

Proteins: 17g

Fats: 21g

Beef Stir-Fry with Vegetable

Portion Size: 2

Duration: 10 min

Ingredients:

8 oz. flank steak, thinly sliced against the grain

2 garlic cloves, minced

1 cup sliced mixed vegetables (such as bell peppers, carrots, and onions)

1 tbsp. vegetable oil

Pepper and Salt

1 tbsp. soy sauce

Instructions:

Preheat your Blackstone griddle to medium heat. Drizzle the vegetable oil over the griddle surface.

Add the sliced beef and minced garlic to the griddle and cook until the beef is browned, about 3 minutes.

Toss in the mixed vegetables and continue to cook for an additional 2 minutes, stirring frequently.

Season with soy sauce, salt, and pepper, and stir to combine all the ingredients evenly.

Serve the beef stir-fry with cooked rice.

Nutrition Facts (1 portion):

Energy: 320 Kcal

Carbs: 12 g

Proteins: 35 g

Fats: 14 g

Chili Con Carne

Portion Size: 2

Duration: 25 min

Ingredients:

1 lb. ground beef

1 can (14 oz.) diced tomatoes, undrained

1 onion, chopped

1 can (15 oz.) kidney beans, drained and rinsed

2 cloves garlic, minced

1 tbsp. chili powder

Pepper and salt

1 tsp. cumin

Instructions:

On the heated Blackstone griddle, cook the ground beef with chopped onion and minced garlic until the beef is fully cooked, about 5-7 minutes. Use your spatula to crumble the beef as it cooks.

Drain any excess fat and return the beef to the griddle.

Stir in the diced tomatoes, kidney beans, chili powder, cumin, salt, and pepper.

Allow the mixture to simmer on the griddle for about 10 minutes, stirring occasionally, until the flavors meld together.

Serve the chili hot, garnished with your choice of toppings.

Nutrition Facts (1 portion):
Energy: 467 Kcal
Carbs: 35 g
Proteins: 36 g
Fats: 23 g

Beef and Mushroom Stroganoff Recipe

Portion Size: 2
Duration: 25 min

Ingredients:
8 oz. beef sirloin, sliced
2 cloves garlic, minced
8 oz. mushrooms, sliced
1/2 cup beef broth
1/2 onion, chopped
1/2 cup sour cream
1 tbsp. vegetable oil
Pepper and Salt
1 tbsp. flour
Cooked egg noodles, for serving

Instructions:

On the Blackstone griddle over medium heat, add the vegetable oil. Once hot, add the beef sirloin, onion, and garlic, cooking until the beef is browned, about 3-4 minutes.

Remove the beef and set aside. In the same area on the griddle, add the mushrooms and cook for about 5 minutes until tender.

In a small bowl, mix the beef broth, sour cream, and flour. Pour this mixture over the mushrooms on the griddle.

Return the beef to the griddle and stir to combine with the mushrooms and sauce. Let it simmer for 10 minutes, stirring occasionally.

Season with salt and pepper as needed. Serve the stroganoff over cooked egg noodles.

Nutrition Facts (1 portion):
Energy: 412 Kcal
Carbs: 16 g
Proteins: 31 g
Fats: 25 g

Beef and Rice Skillet Recipe

Portion Size: 2
Duration: 30 min

Ingredients:
1 lb. ground beef
1 bell pepper, chopped
1 cup beef broth
1 onion, chopped
1 can (14 oz.) diced tomatoes, undrained
2 cloves garlic, minced
1 cup uncooked white rice
1 tsp. chili powder
Pepper and Salt

Instructions:

Begin by cooking the ground beef on the Blackstone griddle over medium heat, adding the chopped onion and minced garlic. Cook until the beef is browned, about 5-7 minutes.

Drain any excess fat and return the beef to the griddle.

In a Skillet add the chopped bell pepper, diced tomatoes with their juice, uncooked rice, beef broth, chili powder, salt, and pepper.

Stir everything together and allow it to come to a boil. Then, reduce the heat to a simmer by lowering the griddle's temperature.

Cover the skillet with a lid or aluminum foil and let it simmer for 18-20 minutes until the rice is cooked and most of the liquid has been absorbed.

Serve the beef and rice skillet hot.

Nutrition Facts (1 portion):

Energy: 580 Kcal

Carbs: 57 g

Proteins: 38 g

Fats: 21 g

French Onion Beef Soup

Portion Size: 2

Duration: 20 min

Ingredients:

1 tbsp olive oil

2 cups beef broth

1/4 cup shredded Gruyere cheese

1 large onion, sliced

1/2 cup red wine

1/2 lb. beef stew meat

1 tsp thyme

Pepper and Salt

1 bay leaf

1 slice of bread

Instructions:

Heat olive oil on the Blackstone griddle. Add the sliced onions and sauté until caramelized.

Add the beef stew meat to the griddle and cook until browned.

Pour in the beef broth, red wine, thyme, bay leaf, salt, and pepper. Bring to a simmer and cook for 30-40 minutes.

Toast the slice of bread on the griddle until crisp.

Place the soup in a bowl suitable for serving. Add the toasted bread on top and sprinkle with shredded Gruyere cheese.

If desired, use a kitchen torch to melt the cheese slightly or serve as is.

Nutrition Facts (1 portion):

Energy: 386 Kcal

Carbs: 17 g

Proteins: 26 g

Fats: 21 g

Classic Meatloaf

Portion Size: 2

Duration: 55 min

Ingredients:

1/2 lb. ground beef

1/4 cup milk

1/4 cup breadcrumbs

1 egg

1 clove garlic, minced

1/4 cup onion, chopped

1 tbsp Worcestershire sauce

Pepper and Salt

Instructions:

Preheat your oven to 370°F.

In a bowl, combine the ground beef, milk, breadcrumbs, egg, chopped onion, minced garlic, Worcestershire sauce, salt, and pepper.

Mix well and shape the mixture into a loaf. Place in a greased loaf pan.

Bake in the oven for 50-60 minutes or until cooked through.

Nutrition Facts (1 portion):

Energy: 317 Kcal

Carbs: 11 g

Proteins: 23 g

Fats: 19 g

Pizza and Pasta Dishes

Spaghetti with Meatballs

Portion Size: 2
Duration: 20 min

Ingredients:
8 oz spaghetti
1/4 cup breadcrumbs
1/4 cup chopped fresh parsley
1/2 lb. ground beef
1 egg
1/4 cup grated Parmesan cheese
1/4 tsp salt
2 tbsp olive oil
24 oz marinara sauce
1 garlic clove, minced
1/4 tsp black pepper

Instructions:
Preheat the Blackstone griddle to medium heat.

In a bowl, combine ground beef, breadcrumbs, parsley, Parmesan, egg, salt, and pepper. Form into half-inch meatballs.

Add olive oil to the griddle and cook meatballs until browned on all sides, about 6 minutes.

Push meatballs to one side of the griddle, add minced garlic, and briefly cook until fragrant.

Pour marinara sauce over meatballs, reduce heat to low, and simmer for 10 minutes.

Meanwhile, cook spaghetti as per the package instructions.

Serve meatballs and sauce over cooked spaghetti.

Nutrition Facts (1 portion):
Energy: 344 Kcal
Carbs: 34 g
Proteins: 17 g
Fats: 15 g

Penne alla Vodka

Portion Size: 2
Duration: 25 min

Ingredients:
8 oz penne pasta
1/2 onion, chopped
1/4 cup vodka
1 tbsp olive oil
1 cup tomato sauce
1 garlic clove, minced
1/2 cup heavy cream
Fresh parsley, chopped
Pepper and salt

Instructions:
Cook penne as per package instructions.

On the griddle, heat olive oil and cook onion and garlic for about 5 minutes.

Add vodka and reduce by half.

Stir in tomato sauce and let simmer. Mix in heavy cream, salt, and pepper.

Add cooked penne to the sauce, toss to coat evenly.

Serve garnished with parsley.

Nutrition Facts (1 portion):
Energy: 305 Kcal
Carbs: 35 g
Proteins: 5 g
Fats: 13 g

Baked Ziti

Portion Size*: 2*
Duration*: 50 min*

Ingredients*:*
8 oz ziti pasta
1 cup ricotta cheese
1/2 onion, chopped
1 jar (24 oz) tomato sauce
1/2 lb. ground beef
1/4 cup grated Parmesan cheese
1 cup shredded mozzarella cheese
1/4 cup chopped fresh parsley
2 garlic cloves, minced
Salt and pepper, to taste
1 cup shredded mozzarella cheese

Instructions*:*
Cook ziti as directed. Brown ground beef with onion and garlic on the griddle for about 7 minutes.
Add tomato sauce to the beef and let simmer.
Mix ricotta, Parmesan, parsley, salt, and pepper in a bowl.
Layer cooked ziti, meat sauce, and ricotta mixture in a baking dish. Repeat layers.
Top with mozzarella cheese.
Bake in a preheated oven at 375°F for 25 minutes.

Nutrition Facts (1 portion)*:*
Energy: 515 Kcal
Carbs: 37 g
Proteins: 31 g
Fats: 27 g

Margherita Pizza

Portion Size*: 2*
Duration*: 15 min*

Instructions*:*
Preheat your Blackstone griddle to 425°F.
Spread pizza sauce over the crust, then add mozzarella cheese and tomato slices.
Sprinkle with basil leaves, salt, pepper, and drizzle with olive oil.
Cook on the griddle until the cheese is bubbly and the crust is crispy, about 10 minutes.

Nutrition Facts (1 portion)*:*
Energy: 205 Kcal
Carbs: 25 g
Proteins: 7 g
Fats: 9 g
Hawaiian Pizza
Portion Size*: 2*
Duration*: 15 min*

Instructions*:*
Preheat Blackstone griddle to 425°F.
Spread pizza sauce over the crust, top with mozzarella cheese, Canadian bacon, and pineapple tidbits.
Season with salt and pepper.
Cook on the griddle until the cheese is bubbly and the crust is crispy, about 12 minutes.

Nutrition Facts (1 portion)*:*
Energy: 225 Kcal
Carbs: 20 g
Proteins: 11 g
Fats: 10 g

Vegetarian Pizza

Portion Size: 2
Duration: 15 min

Instructions:
Preheat Blackstone griddle to 425°F.
Spread pizza sauce over the crust, top with mozzarella cheese, bell pepper, and onion slices.
Drizzle with olive oil, season with salt and pepper.
Cook on the griddle until the cheese is bubbly and the crust is crispy, about 10 minutes.

Nutrition Facts (1 portion):
Energy: 405 Kcal
Carbs: 41 g
Proteins: 18 g
Fats: 18 g
Lemon Butter Pasta with Asparagus
Portion Size: 2
Duration: 15 min

Instructions:
Cook spaghetti as per package instructions.
Add asparagus to boiling water for the last 2-3 minutes of cooking.
In a pan on the griddle, cook butter with lemon juice and garlic.
Add pasta and asparagus to the sauce, toss well.
Season with salt and pepper.

Nutrition Facts (1 portion):
Energy: 302 Kcal
Carbs: 39 g
Proteins: 8 g
Fats: 13 g

Carbonara Spaghetti

Portion Size: 2
Duration: 15 min

Ingredients:
4 oz spaghetti
1/4 cup grated Parmesan cheese
2 slices of bacon, chopped
1 egg
Pepper and salt

Instructions:
Cook the spaghetti on the griddle using a pot with boiling water.
In a separate area, cook the chopped bacon until crispy.
Whisk the egg and Parmesan cheese in a bowl.
Add cooked spaghetti to the griddle with bacon, then add the egg and Parmesan mixture, tossing well.
Season with salt and pepper.

Nutrition Facts (1 portion):
Energy: 406 Kcal
Carbs: 36 g
Proteins: 17 g
Fats: 20 g

Fettuccine Alfredo

Portion Size: 2
Duration: 30 min

Ingredients:
8 oz fettuccine
1/2 cup heavy cream
1/2 cup grated Parmesan cheese
Pepper and salt, to taste

Fresh parsley, chopped

Instructions:

Cook fettuccine on the griddle using a pot with boiling water.

In a pan on the griddle, melt butter and add heavy cream, stirring until combined.

Stir in grated Parmesan until smooth.

Add cooked fettuccine to the sauce, toss, and season with salt and pepper.

Serve garnished with parsley.

Nutrition Facts (1 portion):
Energy: 390 Kcal
Carbs: 24 g
Proteins: 11.5 g
Fats: 18.5 g

Garlic Shrimp Linguine

Portion Size: 2
Duration: 20 min

Ingredients:
8 oz linguine
1/4 cup white wine
1/2 lb. shrimp, peeled and deveined
Fresh parsley, chopped
Pepper and salt

Instructions:

Cook linguine on the griddle using a pot with boiling water.

In a pan, cook minced garlic, then add shrimp and cook until pink.

Add white wine and let it reduce.

Stir in cooked linguine, season, and toss together.

Serve garnished with parsley.

Nutrition Facts (1 portion):
Energy: 345 Kcal
Carbs: 30 g
Proteins: 12 g
Fats: 18 g

Creamy Chicken and Broccoli Alfredo

Portion Size: 2
Duration: 25 min

Ingredients:
8 oz fettuccine
2 tbsp unsalted butter
1 cup broccoli florets
1/2 cup heavy cream
2 cloves of garlic, minced
1/4 cup grated Parmesan cheese
1 lb. cubed, skinless, and boneless chicken breast
- Pepper and salt

Instructions:
Boil pasta in a pot on the griddle.

In a skillet on the griddle, melt butter, and cook chicken until done.

Add broccoli and garlic, cooking until broccoli is tender.

Stir in cream and Parmesan, season with salt and pepper.

Toss cooked pasta in the skillet with the sauce.

Nutrition Facts (1 portion):
Energy: 305 Kcal
Carbs: 24 g
Proteins: 16 g
Fats: 16 g

Pepperoni Pizza

Portion Size*: 2*
Duration*: 15 min*

Instructions*:*

1. Spread pizza sauce over crust.

2. Top with mozzarella and pepperoni.

3. Cook on the griddle until cheese melts and crust is crispy.

Nutrition Facts (1 portion):

Energy: 260 Kcal

Carbs: 19 g

Proteins: 12 g

Fats: 15 g

BBQ Chicken Pizza

Portion Size*: 2*
Duration*: 15 min*

Instructions*:*

Spread BBQ sauce on crust.

Add mozzarella, chicken, and onion.

Cook on the griddle until crust is golden.

Nutrition Facts (1 portion):

Energy: 475 Kcal

Carbs: 49 g

Proteins: 25 g

Fats: 20 g

Four Cheese Pizza

Portion Size*: 2*
Duration*: 15 min*

Instructions*:*

1. Spread tomato sauce on dough.

2. Add mozzarella, Parmesan, and feta.

3. Cook on the griddle until crust is crispy.

Nutrition Facts (1 portion):

Energy: 460 Kcal

Carbs: 32 g

Proteins: 23 g

Fats: 28 g

Tomato and Basil Spaghetti

Portion Size*: 2*
Duration*: 15 min*

Instructions*:*

Cook spaghetti on the griddle.

In a skillet, sauté garlic with red pepper flakes.

Add diced tomatoes and cook until juicy.

Toss cooked spaghetti with the sauce and garnish with basil.

Nutrition Facts (1 portion):

Energy: 238 Kcal

Carbs: 36 g

Proteins: 7 g

Fats: 7 g

Conclusion:

Cooking on a Blackstone Griddle is an exceptional way to bring the delight of outdoor cooking right to your backyard or patio. This cookbook is designed to be your comprehensive guide to mastering the Blackstone Griddle, encompassing everything from its distinct advantages to practical tips and tricks for preparation and cooking. One of the key benefits of cooking on a Blackstone Griddle is its remarkable versatility. Unlike traditional grills, the Blackstone Griddle offers a broad, flat cooking surface that provides precise temperature control, making it ideal for cooking a wide range of dishes to perfection. This makes it a perfect choice for both beginners and seasoned cooks, offering a reliable and diverse cooking experience.

In addition to its versatility, the Blackstone Griddle allows you to explore various cooking methods. From grilling and sautéing to frying and even baking, you can prepare an array of dishes including burgers, pancakes, stir-fries, pizzas, and desserts.

When it comes to prepping and operating your Blackstone Griddle, there are several key tips to keep in mind. First, investing in a high-quality infrared thermometer can be beneficial to accurately gauge the surface temperature of your griddle. This ensures that you cook your food at the ideal heat. Also, understanding the hot zones of your griddle is important as it can affect the outcome of your dishes. Another essential aspect of griddle cooking is maintenance. Regular cleaning is crucial to keep your Blackstone Griddle in top condition and to prevent the build-up of grease and food residues. After each use, we recommend using a griddle scraper to clean the surface thoroughly.

In this cookbook, you'll find a diverse collection of mouth-watering recipes tailored for the Blackstone Griddle. From breakfast and brunch favorites to appetizers, side dishes, salads, and main courses, there's something for everyone. We've also included vegetarian and seafood options to cater to all dietary preferences. This cookbook is meant to inspire you to explore the full potential of your Blackstone Griddle and to equip you with new skills and ideas. Whether you're a griddle novice or a seasoned pro, this book has something to offer. So fire up your Blackstone Griddle, grab your spatulas, and get ready to cook some amazing dishes. Happy griddling!

Made in the USA
Columbia, SC
20 July 2024

260bf388-d211-4295-9a9f-f56ae3ee2bafR02